Prai〈

THE S〈

T0042888

A "Best Music Book of the Year" by *Best Classic Bands*

"John Densmore wrote this book about great artists he's known in the same fashion that he plays drums and lives his life. He understands and demonstrates the value of both silence and sound, space and statement. All the while, he brings us backstage to the parties and personalities that have inspired greatness and been cautionary tales of excess. He proves that it's never too late to grow and these are teachable moments from the life of a master."

—John Doe of X, and coauthor of *Under the
Big Black Sun* and *More Fun in the New World*

"I really enjoyed getting John's unique and insightful view of such an eclectic group of inspiring people."

—Bonnie Raitt, musician and activist

"John Densmore has the heart of a seeker. Always aiming, not for the sparrow, but for the eye of the sparrow in his search for meaning. His compass took him straight to the core of the moment and of the people he was drawn to by his uncanny ability to divine wisdom throughout his fairly frenzied life. It is reaffirming and gratifying to those of us who shared some of the same friends to revisit those unique and original souls."

—Olivia Harrison, author of *George
Harrison: Living in the Material World*

"A joyful history lesson for music geeks."   —*SPIN*

"[It's] fascinating to read this veteran musician's thoughts…these reflections should strike a resonant chord in any aficionado of the arts."

—*All About That Jazz*

Also by John Densmore

*Riders on the Storm: My Life with Jim
Morrison and The Doors*
*The Doors: Unhinged: Jim Morrison's Legacy
Goes on Trial*

THE SEEKERS

Meetings with Remarkable Musicians
(and Other Artists)

JOHN DENSMORE

hachette
BOOKS

New York

Copyright © 2020 by John Densmore

Foreword © 2020 Viggo Mortensen
Jacket illustration and design © Obey Giant Art, Inc. / Shepard Fairey
John Densmore cover illustration source © Jeff Katz Photography
Cover copyright © 2020 by Hachette Book Group, Inc.

Hachette Book Group supports the right to free expression and the value of copyright. The purpose of copyright is to encourage writers and artists to produce the creative works that enrich our culture.

The scanning, uploading, and distribution of this book without permission is a theft of the author's intellectual property. If you would like permission to use material from the book (other than for review purposes), please contact permissions@hbgusa.com. Thank you for your support of the author's rights.

Hachette Books
Hachette Book Group
1290 Avenue of the Americas
New York, NY 10104
HachetteBooks.com
Twitter.com/HachetteBooks
Instagram.com/HachetteBooks

First Trade Paperback Edition: November 2021
First Hardcover Edition: November 2020

Published by Hachette Books, an imprint of Perseus Books, LLC, a subsidiary of Hachette Book Group, Inc. The Hachette Books name and logo is a trademark of the Hachette Book Group.

The Hachette Speakers Bureau provides a wide range of authors for speaking events. To find out more, go to www.hachettespeakersbureau.com or call (866) 376-6591.

The publisher is not responsible for websites (or their content) that are not owned by the publisher.

Print book interior design by Amy Quinn

Library of Congress Control Number: 2020942877

ISBNs: 9780306846236 (hardcover); 9780306846229 (e-book);
       9780306846243 (paperback)

Printed in the United States of America

LSC-C

Printing 1, 2021

To All the Sonic Warriors (music lovers)
who ride the Music of the Spheres

Contents

Seekers All

An artist, She's a real artist. He's a unique artist. Artists are like that. Not like you and me. They feel things, they see things, they understand things in different ways than most people do. Painters, drummers, sculptors, singers, conductors, directors, designers, poets, actors, dancing masters, performers, seekers all. They are sensitive, they see underneath, they see beyond, they see the big picture, they notice the smallest detail. We admire artists, and we don't trust them. The rest of the world gets on with its business while artists daydream and criticize people who actually get things done. They live in their own world, and they should mind their own affairs, stick to what they know. What makes artists so special anyway?

Nothing.

Nothing at all. No more special than you. Each of us has got their own. Each and every one, through our particular way of observing and listening, of being in the world, is free to interpret and communicate what is happening around us. There is no need to be considered or to consider oneself an "artist," in the sense that we conventionally and exclusively use the term, in order to weigh what happens to us in the course of our lives, in order to record in our minds what our experiences mean to us, to decide what attracts and repels us, to relate to and communicate, if and as we choose to, what we find meaningful. Children do not separate themselves as artists or non-artists. Why should adults do so?

You are alive, you receive. You may fine-tune your hearing, you may work on your rhythm, your timing, and find the right moment to dip your toes in the river. Once your skin gets used to the temperature, you may find yourself wading in deeper, maybe going under all the way to your chin. You might have to give it a few tries before getting that far. You don't have to swim. There's nothing to know. You can get out anytime you like. Just sit onshore and watch how others disappear under the surface and come up somewhere else. Watch the rain drops on the gently flowing ripples, if they come. Feel the sun's warmth, if it shines. Get goosebumps, if you do. See what you see, make that picture for yourself. That's all it is, being an artist. Don't ever swim, if it isn't your thing, don't go near the water. Stand on a hilltop, behind a tree, hearing others splash and laugh. No one even needs to know you were there. You understand, you sense as much as anyone else does in their own personal way, whether you're near or far. You can simply imagine being at the bottom, you can count the minnows and tadpoles, the sinking leaves as they swirl around you. You spin at your own speed and dance to the beat you carry as you drift with the current, allowing yourself to float away. You comprehend, already creating, already leaving your mark, even if at first you

can't

hear

keep

listening

to the melody

come up

in a drop

that runs

across the wall

hangs

on the doorknob

sing

together

across
the city
squeeze
a note
that stays
in your fist
pulling
your hair

Unnameable
unknowable
unreasoning
trusting
trading
tuning
tinted
windows

When
did
sound
start
was
there
ever
none?
its absence
unimaginable
its very thought
makes

noise
we begin
and
end
a murmur
risen
from the water
that brought us
keeps us
afloat
lingering
joining
infinite
song
stream

Ensuing
harmony
however
faint
understated
our inevitable
participation
outlasts us
every
echo
imagined
recorded
somewhere
every

piece

variation

remembered

rephrased

desired

unwritten

forgot

unplayed

as time

expands

contracts

reinterprets

resuscitates

incessant hum

we accompany

consciously

or not

VIGGO MORTENSEN

Acknowledgments

First I want to thank Ben Schafer for his editorial skills and his great ear for music. Second, my soul mate Ildiko von Somogyi. Third, Andrea Cagan for her masterful editing eyes. Cynthia Buck for excellent copyediting. Shepard Fairey for the extraordinary cover. He obviously loves music. Jeff Katz for the use of his beautiful cover photo. John Logan for all his help with photo and lyric licenses. Cary Odes for his tech and friendship. Sam Joseph for suggesting I write about all these great artists I've met. Jeff Jampol for management guidance.

Finally, a little story: There's a tradition among the *real* gurus that the disciple must try really hard before the teaching is allowed to come out. There is a myth related to this about the mystic Gurdjieff that just might be based in truth. It is said that Gurdjieff would tell his pilgrims to meet him in a bar at such and such a time, only to quickly tell everyone that they would be going to another bar instead. That weeded out half or more of the flock. Then, after one drink, he insisted that they go to a third tavern. It was getting very late in the evening at this point, and only a few stragglers were left. Gurdjieff lifted his glass and said something like, "Let's get down to it. I'm ready to talk." The Master showed the jewels only to those who were really thirsty.

So in that tradition, even if this latest tome of mine sells very little, I will try (I'm still a work in progress) to be pleased that those of you who labored over my scribbling actually "got it." Thanks so much for the effort.

Introduction

THE TIME HAS NEVER BEEN MORE RIGHT FOR WRITING A BOOK that elucidates my lifelong commitment to the arts and creativity. It has been proven that music and arts therapy heals post-traumatic stress disorder (PTSD), not to mention that the arts make *all* of us feel better. To illuminate this urgent and timely issue, I have turned to a nearly century-old book for inspiration: the Greek-Armenian mystic G. I. Gurdjieff's 1927 classic book, *Meetings with Remarkable Men*. This widely influential spiritual memoir has a cultlike status that has inspired generations of artists and writers, including Sting, Kate Bush, *Mary Poppins* author P. L. Travers, acclaimed filmmaker Alejandro Jodorowsky, and Peter Gabriel (who named his world-music record label Real World Records after Gurdjieff's *Views from the Real World*).

Gurdjieff started working on the manuscript of *Meetings with Remarkable Men*, originally written in Russian, in 1927, revising it several times over the coming years. The author reminisces about "remarkable men" he has known, including his father, the Armenian priest Pogossian, his friend Prince Yuri Lubovedsky (a Russian prince interested in spiritualism and occultism), and five other sages. Gurdjieff describes these characters and weaves their stories into his account of his own travels. He calls this group the "Seekers of Truth" because ultimately they cooperate in searching for spiritual texts and masters wherever they can be found (mostly in central Asia). Most of these "Seekers of Truth" do in fact find truth in the form of a suitable spiritual destiny.

Inspired by this idea, I've assembled my own group of what I would call musical masters who achieved their mystical destiny through sound—from Ravi Shankar to Patti Smith, Jim Morrison to Janis Joplin, Bob Marley to Gustavo Dudamel, Lou Reed to Van Morrison, Jerry Lee Lewis to my dear late Doors bandmate Ray Manzarek. Just as painters "see" the world, musicians' primary compass through life is their ears. Like my colleagues, I "hear" the world. The one constant thread through my life so far is that I have been constantly fed and nourished by music.

I would like to take readers along on a quest to illuminate the creative process, using storytelling and unique access to show how it happens. *The Seekers* will allow you to join me in exploring timeless ideas and addressing universal questions as I go backstage and into the lives and minds of these great artists.

As Sting sang in "Secret Journey" (his 1981 song inspired by Gurdjieff's book), he saw himself as a lonely man on a private quest to make some sense of the mysteries of life and the elusive nature of love. Sting expresses the yearning need to reach a greater understanding with the help of a wise teacher, a holy man of sorts, who would guide him and whose words would continue to reverberate throughout his life. Like Sting, I'm Ronald Colman in the film *Lost Horizon*, trying to find Sam Jaffe (the High Lama) in all of these chapters. Great musicians are in love with sound, and their songs can be spiritual texts. Sound is what connects these giants, all of them sonic warriors constantly looking for a new vibration or reinvigorating an old one.

As I introduce readers to the iconic artists in this book, I'll also share some insights I've picked up on how to live creatively on Planet Earth. I think we can get only hints of answers to these questions about how to connect with the muses, because they're ephemeral agents from the other world. The great mythologist Joseph Campbell puts it succinctly: "God is a metaphor which transcends all levels of intellectual thought." But we mortals keep trying, don't we?

Because of my good fortune, I have had the opportunity to meet and interact with some extraordinary people. To be a member of The Doors and have the unusual access I have been afforded is one of the greatest blessings of my life. But what I've learned is that anyone can access the magical moments these gifted artists live in. Whether you have a nine-to-five job, or you sit alone at the piano playing something only you will ever hear, or you're an aspiring artist hungry to learn how these heroes approach their work (like me), this book is a guide for the Seeker in us all.

If beauty is the only real antidote to this modern, crazy world, then, as the mythologist Michael Meade says, "Art is a form of refuge." And if that's true, then we're all refugees. Meade elaborates: "We're all looking for a sanctuary, a place to feel at peace with ourselves and the world." William Blake said that "each day has a moment of eternity waiting for you."

So even if you're not a "professional" musician, you can access the same zone a professional does; you too can open the door (pun intended!) to the other world. I'm not one of the fastest drummers, and fortunately accessing that creative zone is not all about technique either. It's about the heart: when the heart is open, the muses will be attracted and show up. In matters of spirit, the most direct connection is through music. The ancestor spirits want to participate when they sense the presence of feeling instead of logic. So just sing or play an instrument and you will quickly become enchanted. (*Chanson* is the French word for "song.")

As we try to glean everything we can from these icons, notice they have accomplished this elevated status not by pursuing the outer world, but the inner world of sound. Most of these artists certainly *are* idols in the public's eyes, but their initial incentive came not from wanting outward approval, but from an inner desire—an almost unstoppable drive to create something. Beethoven wrote the Ninth Symphony (possibly his greatest) when he was completely deaf. He could only hear it in his head, and the fact that a stagehand had to tap him on the shoulder to signal that it was time to come out for another curtain call after conducting the work is almost unimaginably sad. When composing, Ludwig would put a pencil in his mouth and press it against the piano to feel the vibrations because he couldn't hear them. But his deafness also points to the richness of his inner sonic life. In the words of the great sage Ram Dass, "The quieter you are, the more you hear."

The muse is very psychic, and as I said, she will come when the heart is open, but a well-crafted vessel attracts her big-time. Sometimes she blows the circuitry like in Janis Joplin's case.

Fueled by substance abuse, the muse will devastate the vessel and wound the soul. But there are also very disciplined artists, such as the impeccable Ravi Shankar, whose vessel is as solid as a rock. Bob Marley is somewhere in between. He has the right amount of craft that is needed for his message. That's the thing about technique: you need just enough to get across your gift (and we've all come into this world with a unique gift to bring), but you can have too much. That is to say, you can be seduced by learning to go faster and faster, but as the great American poet Robert Bly used to say, "slow equals soul."

I feel so blessed to have been in the presence of these great artists, some for a moment, some for an extended time over many years. Some have broken on through to the other side, while some are still here in their physical form. So this is my thank-you, my tip of the hat to these artists and musicians, classically trained or barely schooled at all. I've thrown in a couple of writers as well because, in my opinion, they're looking for music in between the sentences.

The passion of what these icons are trying to say comes through in spades; they sparkle like diamonds in the rough or fully polished. That sparkle is the thread that tugs on our humanity and reminds us that we come from the same family and that everyone is struggling to make sense out of their lives. And everyone can glean inspiration from these artists. The food they offer is so rich that only a little can be savored for a lifetime. I hope you get as much as I have out of this feast.

Chapter One

Margret (Peggy) Mary Walsh

Survival

Drawing or painting on a canvas is frozen music.

How could I not start with my mom? She wasn't a musician—just a force of nature whose life would span almost the entire twentieth century. My dad was quiet, and Mom was not. She loved music so much that she even let me set up and play my cacophonous drums in the living room. My parents' musical tastes were eclectic—some good, like Beethoven, some not so good, like Mantovani.

Survival was Margaret Mary's thing. It was the leitmotif (a repeating musical theme) throughout her life. She had four siblings, but at a young age endured losing two of them, her older

1

sisters. Assimilating those deaths as a kid barely into her teens must have shaken her to the core. As my cousin Jim wisely said, "Hearing about the death of her sister May possibly made your mom fill space with talk."

She got through all the struggles by painting. Drawing or painting on a canvas is frozen music. There's space between the images, as there's space between sounds in music. Getting her diploma from Chouinard Art Institute in Los Angeles, Peggy Margaret was obsessed with putting something on the blank canvas. Signing all her work with the name "Margret" (she took the "a" out to make the name unique), she could do figurative drawing quite well, but eventually fell in love with abstract.

I wasn't that crazy about her work, but I knew that it saved her life. When Dad passed, I thought that, after forty years of marriage, Mom would soon follow suit. She didn't. Instead, she blossomed. "When I have pain, I paint," she'd say. I didn't understand most of her paintings, but I understood the gift bestowed on her by doing them: painting stopped time. In my opinion, painting was her *real* religion. She thrived until the age of ninety-four, when she finally put down her brush and died.

So I'm hoping I received some of those survival genes. She loved music and allowed me to take piano lessons when I was eight years old. Peggy Margret encouraged me to practice. She even threatened to take away those lessons if I didn't practice more. I loved the piano. I loved fooling around doing arpeggios (broken-up three-note chords) up and down the keyboard. I would do them for hours, pretending I was a concert pianist. It was then that Mom would come in my room and say, "Practice your lesson or no more lessons." She was right, but my tendency to drift off into my own improvisations was an indication of things to come. Jazz.

There was freedom in changing the written compositions, repeating a phrase or inventing a new one to go with what was on the page. Then I'd have to get back to learning more scales and legit compositions. You have to eventually intuit how much woodshedding (practice) you should do, and how much free play you should allow to come in. That balance is the key to finding your own musical uniqueness.

Speaking of unique, I used to have a pet parakeet that I would let out of its cage, and he'd sit on my finger or shoulder. One day while "Bill" was pecking at my neck from his shoulder perch, I walked over to the piano and sat down. He certainly had heard me play while sitting in his cage and had sung along when I put more effort into it. I thought that this time I should play soft, because he was so close to the upright piano. I lightly started arpeggios in a major key (a major key is a "positive" sound). Bill joined right in, and so after a few minutes I put my finger out in front of my shoulder for him to jump on. As usual, he quickly obliged. Then I gently set him down on the white keys near the top of the keyboard. I started playing again, which didn't upset him at all.

This became our routine—the two of us enjoying the sonorous sounds of the eighty-eight keys. Sometimes he would walk up and down the keys. Sometimes he would shit on the keys. I'd clean it up right away; I didn't want mushy keys, and I certainly didn't want to piss off Margaret Mary. Maybe I should have explored music more with my pet bird. We could have been an act on *The Ed Sullivan Show* or Comedy Central. Well, I *was* on Ed Sullivan later in life, but no bird was accompanying me, just a guy in black leather. That, at the time, was a unique wardrobe. Jim should have gotten a cut of the fashion trend he jump-started.

When The Doors were starving, we'd go over to my mom's house and she would make us a spaghetti dinner. This was before Robby was in the band. My dad thought our band name was dumb, but he didn't know the book it was taken from, *The Doors of Perception* by Aldous Huxley. He didn't get that the idea was to open the doors of your mind. Not necessarily with drugs, although that's what the book was about. It could also be done with alcohol. It could be done with meditation. It could even be done with books.

Ray Manzarek and his girlfriend Dorothy would always ask for second helpings of spaghetti. They didn't have the privilege of raiding Ray's parents' fridge, which was an hour south in Manhattan Beach. I was worried how Jim would behave, but he was hungry too, so the vibe was cordial. When I leaned back on the two rear legs of my dining room chair, which I'd been doing for years, Mom didn't hassle me to "sit up," not while my bandmates were around. I still have that table and the set of six chairs, one of which creaks likes crazy from all that leaning back. Once I fell over backwards, which secretly pleased my mom. Lesson not learned.

I would say that she gave me the gift of music vicariously by dragging me to Catholic church, where I was exposed to the sounds played by the mad, drunken Irish organist. Also through her love of hearing music at home. At mass, I told Mom I couldn't stand the smell of the incense, so she let me go up to the balcony where no one sat because Mr. K (with the red nose) played the organ way too loud for the masses. Mom said he got too carried away with the volume pedal. Sitting alone up there with him as he rocked into "Ave Maria," I could feel the low notes shaking my seat, which vibrated my brain into a slight euphoric high.

At home, it was either corny orchestral Muzak or Beethoven played on the box. I resonated with both, but liked the drama of serious classical mo' better. The highs (fortissimo) and lows (pianissimo) of the three Bs (Bach, Beethoven, and Brahms) would later seep into my percussion work. This music was a big gift Mom gave me by encouraging my piano lessons, and it later made my drumming much more musical as well.

As for her "Margarita" nickname, my mom could drink me under the table. She came from the 1950s martini crowd, so she was used to cocktails every night. I came from the '60s pot-smoking, "alcohol is for old people" era. When she got older and I'd take her to a favorite Mexican restaurant, Margret would have several margaritas and definitely get a buzz and talk even *more*. I gave up on keeping up with her. Besides, I was her designated driver and one tequila was enough for the "cheap high" son. She loved the mariachis (Mexican musicians) and struck up a conversation with anyone who would listen. Even if you weren't listening, she'd keep going.

I mentioned the exhausting chatter in my eulogy for her, and got a big laugh when I said that keeping up with ninety-two-year-old "Peggy Margarita" wasn't possible. She's resting in peace now, or maybe she's having an Irish nightcap with Dad. She drove me nuts in my early years, but all the memories are sweet now.

A few days before she passed, my cousin MaryAnn said I'd better make the hour-and-a-half drive up to see her soon, because she was going fast. I said I'd leave right away. Having been up a few days before, I procrastinated, then an hour or so later I finally left for Ventura. When I got there, Peggy Margret was asleep. She hadn't crossed over yet; she would live another day, but she would not be waking up again. Now I knew I should have left home immediately.

The caregivers said that she'd been up at 3:00 a.m. the night before and that was why she'd fallen asleep so early. They had obviously told her I was on my way because she was lying in her bed, all decked out with turquoise earrings, a turquoise necklace, and slightly smeared lipstick. A ninety-four-year-old woman still wanting to look good for her son is an image that will stay with me forever.

Chapter Two

Robert Armour

The Twinkle

What's in the eye reveals the soul.

Mr. Armour was a nerdy flute player and my junior high school music teacher. In fact, all of us musicians were nerds. It wasn't "cool" yet to be a musician. Jocks were cool. They wore letterman sweaters with the symbol of their sport (football, baseball, track) in the middle of the "U" for University High in West Los Angeles. That's where I eventually went after Daniel Webster Junior High.

Of course, back then, if you wore a sweater with tennis rackets in the middle of the "U" for Uni High, you might be gay. And we didn't have that word back then. We had a much more derogatory word that started with an "f." I didn't have to worry about other students thinking I was gay: I was the last man on the tennis team and was never asked to play a game in competition, so I couldn't letter. Mostly I hit the ball against the wall.

But I was obsessed with music. After I began piano lessons at age eight, I took to the instrument immediately. I couldn't get enough of it and was already leaning toward jazz. I preferred improvising on compositions rather than learning new ones. Playing them over and over, changing little things here and there, put me into a trance as time seemed to stop moving. I was still too young to realize that art releases us from the trap of time.

When I got to Webster, I wanted to play in the symphonic band, orchestra, jazz ensemble—any musical group they had. And I really didn't care what instrument I played. I knew they didn't have a space for a pianist in the band or the orchestra, so I chose clarinet. The trombone seemed interesting to me, the way you slide part of the instrument with your left hand. I liked the shiny gold look of it too, but I'd heard my parents play Benny Goodman records, and clarinet seemed more "cool" than trombone. Maybe girls would like me if I played clarinet.

Alas, I had braces on my teeth at the time, and the orthodontist said, "No, you can't play clarinet! We're trying to push your teeth back . . . that instrument will push them out!" I asked Mr. Armour, who was also my homeroom teacher, what he thought. "Well, John, we need drummers for the band and the orchestra." That was appealing because drums have a built-in "cool" vibe.

I had to start with the bass drum, a solo bass drum. Then I learned the cymbal parts. I was working my way up to the snare, which played the more sophisticated, intricate rhythms. Mr. Armour encouraged me to be patient. Later I realized that I had developed an intimate knowledge of each of the elements of the drum set, and all put together they represented the entire world of percussion. "Traps" was the jazz slang for the set, because all the elements "trapped" together.

My musical mentor also encouraged me to take private lessons. "If you really want to improve fast, that's the way to go," Mr. Armour said. I've gotta hand it to my parents: they not only put up the dough but occasionally tolerated loud drums in their house. I say "occasionally" because most of the time I was encouraged to practice on a black rubber "drum pad," which was lame. The stick bounced back like it was hitting a drum, but it made no sound.

After finally graduating to playing timpani (kettle drums) in the orchestra, I found it thrilling to execute the dramatic rolls at the end of symphonies. I would be counting bars, waiting for my time to come in and watching Mr. Armour, with his Richard Nixon hairdo, conduct with his little baton. He was tall and commanding at the podium. Anything involving music put a twinkle in his eye. In fact, he seemed to always have that twinkle, and I think it came from his love of music. As the California visionary educator Paul Cummins said, "The living example of the teacher's excitement for the subject becomes a yardstick by which the student measures life. The teacher's energy represents a vital ingredient the student wishes to discover within himself."

The power of The Doors came from the ensemble, a lesson I learned from Mr. Armour. It doesn't matter if you're a four-piece rock band or a forty-piece orchestra. The key to the magic is every player serving the ensemble, with everyone listening intently to each other. The whole equals more than the sum of its parts. I got that message as a kid in the junior high school orchestra. And gosh, if different cultures respected each other in that way, we'd have a bunch of societies acting in concert as a global orchestra playing different, but harmonious, sounds.

Many many years later, I went back to visit Daniel Webster Junior High School, which had become extremely run-down. My photo was still up on the wall in the musical "Hall of Fame" section, but it was clear that not much money was going into keeping the music building up to date, let alone the entire campus. I had a few words with the new music teacher. He said that my years at the school, back in the day with Mr. Armour, had been a golden period. Worn-out musical equipment or not, it was the passion emanating from the nerdy flute player that made all the difference.

Musicians are ambassadors to the hidden world inside everyone. To Robert Armour, the flute was that little bird ("a little bird told me . . . ") inside everyone who knows the song line of each individual life. Mr. Armour definitely lit my musical fire and held up a flashlight illuminating my future path. Thank you, Robert A.

Chapter Three

Fred Katz

Professor
at Large

Teaching by example inspires the most inspiration.

I first saw him at the Lighthouse in Hermosa Beach. I was seventeen and making another pilgrimage to the famous jazz mecca. Chico Hamilton, who was already one of my heroes, had his quintet sequestered onstage. Later, I would "borrow" Chico's ride cymbal style for the Doors' song "The End," but back then my teenage mind was trying to wrap around the concept of a cello player in a jazz group. Who was this bespectacled, Hassidic-looking dude up there? And could cello players improvise? As it turned out, Fred Katz's entire life was one giant improv. But that afternoon (the Lighthouse always had Sunday jazz matinees), the cello player played the head (the melody line) of all the songs and also improvised his ass off via bowing, plucking, and singing his solos. We ate it up.

I was born in Santa Monica, not too far from Hollywood, and attended San Fernando Valley State College—now Cal State Northridge. I had first majored in music, but thought I could never make a living at that, so I switched to business. But now, several years after that night at the Lighthouse, I was looking around at other courses. The first of my two memoirs, *Riders on the Storm: My Life with Jim Morrison and The Doors*, explains it best:

> That spring I changed my major several times at Valley State. I knew I was going to hate business, but I had taken it because I figured you had to know it if you were going to eat. I got D's . . . I wouldn't listen to my real feelings. I was letting other people influence me. So this time I made my own absurd decision. I like people. I wanted to help people. Maybe Sociology was for me. But I hated that too.

Then I noticed a course called Ethnological Music. What the hell was that? I considered myself a musician, "ethnological" must mean different cultures, and the course was offered in the anthropology division. I looked closer at the course description. Holy shit! The professor is Fred Katz! Could that be the same dude I saw years ago playing cello in the Chico Hamilton Quintet?

I checked the biography section of the school catalog, and sure enough, it was him. *I'll be damned*, I thought. I tried to enroll in the course immediately, but there was a long waiting list. The next semester I finally got in, and Professor Katz was incredibly charming and fascinating. No wonder Ethnological Music was the most popular class on campus—not because it was an easy A, which it was, but because Katz was just *so* interesting. *Riders* elaborates:

> I got the sense that he [Professor Katz] had been out in the world and knew about life. He would have fellow musicians [flutist Paul Horn] come in and perform for the class, so one actually got a glimpse of the real world. Of course, the administrators "voluntarily" let him go a couple of years after I left. Too far out!

Not too long after they let Fred go, the campus erupted in student protests.

It seems that the people who run our colleges don't really have their finger on the pulse of their constituents. Their attitude reminds me of the late Supreme Court Justice Antonin Scalia. He wrung his hands over the legalization of gay marriage and blamed it on the hippies of half a century earlier, for apparently having a disrespectful attitude toward marriage. Scalia was appointed by Ronald Reagan, who also hated the hippies. As I write this in 2020, students (those damn young people again) are protesting the tuition hikes at all the University of California campuses.

You could see what frustrated the college administrators fifty years ago: Professor Katz wouldn't stay on point and just said what was on his mind. But the vitality and enthusiasm he had for life were reeking from all of his pores, and that was the greatest lesson one could ever receive.

I still have one more year to go (thirty units) before I can get my BA in anthropology. But I don't think I'm going back. I did go back to visit Fred Katz when he was in his nineties. I had noticed in the *Los Angeles Times* that the very respectable Skirball Cultural Center was hosting a return, after twenty years, of one of Fred's living room concerts. I was in the second row. Decorated with chairs and sofas, the stage had a living room ambiance if there ever was one. The set mimicked Professor Katz's actual living room, where for many years he had hosted jam sessions.

Back in the day, classical people showed up. After all, in his early years, Fred studied with Pablo Casals. Jazz people showed up. After all, Fred had played with Dexter Gordon, Charles Mingus, Lester Young, Lena Horne, Tony Bennett, Gerry Mulligan, Ken Nordine, and Buddy Collette, to name a few. Also guitarist Jim Hall, Paul Horn, Eric Dolphy, Gábor Szabó, and Charles Lloyd, to name a few more.

The Maestro jammed a little on his cello, sat down on the couch, and began to rap. The Man loved to rap. He thanked us for showing up to the rehearsal for his ninety-second birthday. He told jokes. He played some more music. The warmth in the room was palpable. It was as if he'd invited all two hundred of us into his living room. One could understand what frustrated the college administration about Fred Katz: his greatest teaching was simply *who* he was.

At the end of the festivities, I waited for a bit, then went up and reintroduced myself. Professor Katz started shouting, "Hey! It's the Doors guy! John! The drummer!" That was flattering, and rather embarrassing. But if it made my mentor happy to see me, it made me happy. We said our goodbyes, and I drove home full of spirit.

A month or so later, Fred's spirit flew higher than ever. Supernovas were blasting the news: "A great musical spirit is now everywhere! He's in the ether! He's in the ocean! You can tap into him anywhere. He's totally available! You don't have to buy a ticket. His love and wisdom are boundless! A lover of life is now a guardian angel! Call on him . . . he always returns. He'll text all of you back through sound waves."

Chapter Four
Elvin Jones
The Edge

On the outskirts, you can see the whole.

When I was a teenage drummer, I stumbled onto John Coltrane's records and sensed something magical. I was too young to understand what attracted me. But I knew that the constant "searching" in Elvin Jones's drumming put me in a trance. Jones used rhythm to access eternity.

First and foremost for drummers, or any musician for that matter, is having a strong sense of time, being able to feel the internal steady tempo. Without it, they won't be able to get into that hypnotic state of timelessness. If you can't feel the tempo, flashy technique isn't going to save you. The jazz giant Thelonious Monk emphasized the point perfectly when he wrote down a list of the ten most important things a musician needs to be good. *First* on that list was a good sense of time, *"especially if you're* not *the drummer!"* That was a really smart comment. Monk knew that a sax player can solo like crazy, but that it won't work without the inner metronome. If you don't have it, the feeling would be like lying on a gurney in the hospital, and seeing your EKG digital readout fluctuate up and down when it's supposed to be steady.

Elvin Jones, my mentor, my main man, "broke on through to the other side" on May 18, 2004, but he laid it down on drums so heavy, so strong, that his pulse will be felt for centuries. Elvin Jones, the polyrhythmic "jazz machine" and the motor behind the Trane, crossed the tracks. He blazed a new path for all the rest of us timekeepers. He was the first to really free up the job of clockwork, improvising continually, but never sacrificing a strong sense of pulse.

For drummers, the steady tempo is everything. No matter what you're playing rhythmically, if the pulse isn't implied no one is going to care or be moved. Native Americans say that the powwow drum used in their dances is a steady, singular rhythm because it is the heartbeat of Mother Earth. We drummers all know that our mother's heartbeat was the first instrument we heard. If your rhythmic pulse falters in the least, the ensemble you're playing with would fear that their mother's heartbeat just stopped, and they were still inside the womb (song). When your beats have a consistent feel, the listener is comforted and can groove to the sound and enjoy the warm amniotic fluids— the ultimate "homeland security"—of the song.

As a species, we've all been trying to get back to that womb. That's why rhythm makes us move and dance. When people "groove" to jazz music or dance to reggae or hip-hop, they always move on the one—the first beat of each bar of music. It's like our bodies have an electrical hookup to the pulse of the song, the heartbeat.

The first time I met Elvin was in 1963. I nervously showed my fake ID from Tijuana to the doorman at Shelly's Manne Hole, a jazz club in Hollywood. He looked at it, gave me one last glance that said, *Yeah, it's fake*, and let me in to see my hero.

At sixteen, I had already pored over all of Coltrane's Impulse! LPs, feeding my ears like the music was candy. It was like the musical gods were offering up hot fudge sundaes with each album. My autobiography *Riders on the Storm* captures the obsession: "Anytime I would drop the needle on a Coltrane record, the bellowing, driving energy would make me imagine I was actually inside drummer Elvin Jones's body. The tempo pulsed in my veins." After dissecting every nuance of his style on records (down to his moaning between quarter notes), I was about to make my first flesh-and-blood contact with Elvin, the first of several occasions (unbeknownst to me) to come. He sat behind one of the greatest jazz quartets in the history of the art form, and he did it with that huge grin. The Beatles hadn't hit yet, and Elvin Jones was my muse.

Coltrane stood up front, but I was fixated on "The Man" sitting in the back. I listened in awe as Elvin played one beat while implying another, or played both at the same time, which stretches the brain cells and creates tension. Shyamdas, the late Kirtan singer, used to say that you have to worship the Tal (the time, in Hindi) and always have your awareness on where the one is. Elvin did that and could still churn rhythms like an eggbeater, serving up multiple meals within every four bars. And he did it with a big smile. His rhythms were perpetually on the edge, like he was just about to fall into his drum set (but never did). The pulse was always there, the connection to the divine.

Elvin's constant "conversation" with Coltrane later inspired me to try to have a musical dialogue with Jim Morrison. It was Jones's loose way of playing that gave me the courage to literally stop the steady rhythm on "When the Music's Over" during Morrison's rap about the earth and just jab at my kit (drum set) in quick expressive grunts. My intuition eventually told me to go back to the groove, like when pianist McCoy Tyner came back in after one of Elvin and Coltrane's intense exchanges.

Between sets at the Manne Hole, I went back to the bathroom, not because I had to relieve myself, but because I knew it was right next to the dressing room. I heard voices and laughter from behind the wall. I occupied myself washing my hands until I heard the voices drifting out into the hallway. Then I spun around and, wiping my hands on my pants, opened the door.

Coltrane was standing right in front of me, looking at who was coming out of the bathroom. My reverence immediately told me to "chill," so I avoided eye contact and just motioned that the head was free. But Trane didn't go in. He just walked by, headed for the stage. I noticed that everyone sort of quieted down when he passed. Then Elvin walked by, looked over, and *nodded at me.* When the last set was over, I lingered again in the back, where I heard Elvin say to Trane, "Hotel, hotel," which I took to mean he wanted to go to his room. I repeated the phrase over and over to my friends the next few days. They thought I was nuts.

The next time I witnessed the muse being channeled via Elvin's direct line to the sun was a show at UCLA's Royce Hall. The most seminal jazz band ever was now becoming much more popular, but Coltrane's continual probing of "the new" and his sense of integrity were pushing the quartet to sonic areas that made some people uncomfortable. Not me. At Royce Hall, I sat in the front row as they played one song that went on for forty-five minutes. Burning with fury, half the audience left before the musicians finished. They couldn't take it. The new fans just didn't understand. Knowing his history, I ate up all of John's experimental excursions into space. If he hadn't helped define bebop and "cool" jazz with Miles Davis, he wouldn't have had permission to go "outside." It was actually "inner" space, as exemplified in one of his titles: "Chasin' the Trane." In the middle of the long tune, pianist McCoy Tyner laid out, leaving the rhythm section, bassist Jimmy Garrison, and Elvin to face off with their leader. Coltrane turned around and, with his back to us, entered into a duel with my percussion master. It was twenty minutes of the most emotional catharsis I've ever heard out of any musician. The two of them indeed "left this world," like the old Johnny Mercer tune "Out of This World," which they had covered on one of their albums. You see, CBS, NBC, and ABC is not the world. The real world is behind the world, as the Irish would say. The real world, like nature, is infinite.

Elvin's stamina was a perfect match for the tenor player. He looked like someone you wouldn't want to meet in a back alley, but also contained in his vibe was love. I knew that stamina would eventually take Elvin out; a commitment to hearing every single beat your entire life will dissipate your energy. Broad shoulders on top of buff arms, it seemed he went to the gym every day, which he did, via working out on his kit. A friend of mine who saw Elvin play just before he died remarked on how sad it was to see that energy so diminished.

The thought of Elvin Jones up there on the stage, practically passing out but insisting on doing what he did best, hurts me deep inside. On the other hand, we all pay for what we do, whether it's drumming, playing violin, painting, sitting in front of a computer, or jackhammering; we can't escape occupational hazards. But if what you're doing gives you a sense of agelessness, who cares? I've had some recent issues with my back, the result of the way I slumped over my kit for fifty years. But if I'd done it differently, it wouldn't have sounded the same, and I played it how I heard it. No regrets.

John Coltrane's exposure to Indian and African classical music played a part in the ensemble's view that some music is not a means to an end but rather a way to further one's spiritual journey. Critics were calling their new direction "grotesque," "willful ugliness," and "gobbledygook." Ironically, however, Trane's audiences increased, and I was right there for the ride. He put listeners in a trance, then took them for a meditative Trane ride. It was like being slipped a "sonic" drug and getting on the sound train for an excursion. Some listeners might prefer the dining car, where JC served up beautiful ballads like "After the Rain," while others liked it best up near the engine, where they could get the very intense "Chasin' the Trane." Some even liked to go where all of us drummers ride: the caboose. It's quite bouncy back there.

If you surrendered to the music, the effect was similar to the "possession" that arises in some churches, and it also expressed the anger and rage over the political state of affairs at that time, and over racism in particular. The civil rights movement was in full throttle, and JC had his finger on the pulse of the nation. After the Ku Klux Klan bombed a church in Alabama, Coltrane wrote the powerful "Alabama." He patterned the song after the Rev. Martin Luther King's eulogy for the four African American girls who were killed in the blast.

Coltrane was also an influence at this time on minimalist American classical composers such as La Monte Young and Philip Glass. Musically, there is a close parallel between minimal and modal. Both styles leave a lot of space for the listener to wander around in.

It made sense to me when I learned later that Coltrane, an insatiable music lover, had struck up a friendship in the late 1950s with the sitar master Ravi Shankar. Now there's music that makes a lot of space. Ravi's music (which I talk about a few chapters down the road) has endured because of the sense it projects of not being time-bound. Their discussions and jam sessions educated JC in the science of sound, showing him that musical riffs reflect specific states of consciousness. His wife Alice put it eloquently: "He was questioning whether it's possible to realize Truth through sound."

His drummer was already there. Elvin's complex playing simultaneously captured the past, the present, and the future. One of Coltrane's LPs was called *OM*, which in Sanskrit means "to sound." It also is defined as "all that exists beyond the three forms of time (past, present, future), included in one sound." Elvin implied that from moment to moment. If John Coltrane was obviously searching for Truth, Elvin Jones had already found it through rhythm.

Swami Satchidananda, the Indian guru who spoke at the beginning of the Woodstock Music Festival in 1969, confirmed Elvin and Coltrane's search by saying:

There are certain mystical sounds (OM) which the Sanskrit terminology says are the bijakshara, or the "seed words." Music is a celestial sound and it is the sound that controls the whole universe, not atomic vibrations. Sound energy, sound power, is much, much greater than any other power in this world.

In an interview, Coltrane said that he knew there were bad forces that brought suffering. He said he wanted to be a force for good.

It makes me think of my instrument, drums, used to inspire patriotic reverie to get the soldiers to kill their fellow human beings. Another master drummer named Jones, as in Jo, told a young player, "Do not beat the drum, play the drum . . . the drum is a woman." Certainly John Coltrane's drummer also taught us that drumming is more than the soundtrack for war, more than the beat that allows us to dance. Elvin took it to the highest level possible. Reflecting on the Coltrane years, he said: "We articulated all of our collective knowledge up to that point—making it into a cohesive sound within that context. It expressed the way we felt spiritually, emotionally, and intellectually. We didn't have to converse . . . everything was telepathic."

After the UCLA performance, people were allowed to wander up onstage, so yours truly sheepishly played the role of groupie. This wasn't a rock show, so fans didn't have to climb the Berlin Wall to get to an artist. I still lacked the nerve to actually *say* anything to my teacher, so I just watched as Elvin used a hammer to remove the nails he'd pounded right into the floor to keep his bass drum from sliding. At times the man played hard. I just lurked around near his drum set, stealing glances at my teenage idol. Eventually he became a friend, and his musical style is the one I emulate the most to this day.

My next physical contact with Elvin Jones was many years later. In the '80s, Coltrane had died and Elvin's Jazz Machine was initiating lots of new young players. I was in New York, and I ventured down to Slugs on the Lower East Side. (Slugs was the jazz club where trumpeter Lee Morgan was shot by his wife.) With a red-brick wall as the stage backdrop, Elvin's sound was projected louder than ever. He rarely wore a jacket, as a lot of jazz musicians did, because his bulging arms would rip the seams. I could tell once again that his music was a little too much for some of the patrons, but my own craving for his rhythms was satiated for a while.

I thought back to early Doors rehearsals where we fashioned the solos in "Light My Fire" after some of the chord changes in "My Favorite Things." Coltrane had taken a corny Broadway tune from *The Sound of Music* and made it his own. Apparently, Elvin had fed me, because the esteemed music critic Greil Marcus had this to say about my playing on "Light My Fire":

All across Manzarek's solo there is a beast to one side, John Densmore, who with the constant, pushing insistence of tumbling drums, could be eating the music whole, spitting it back. At unexpected moments he pulls back, pulls Manzarek with him, his sound suddenly full of open spaces, and you hear the stick hit the snare as a single event. With Krieger's solo he is more circumspect, as if the beast isn't sure what species of animal it's now faced with, as if it's willing to wait to find out. As the passage goes on, so fluidly from Krieger, Densmore repeats the single snare shot he used to kick the song off, the first thing you hear, its echo immediately swallowed by Manzarek's opening fanfare, and, at the end, almost the last thing you hear. From start to finish, Densmore's hand is on the wheel, that's why everyone else sounds so free.

I *know* I got this from jazz, and I am so grateful.

In 1995, I caught Jones at the Vine Street Bar & Grill, a jazz club just a couple of blocks from the old Manne Hole in Hollywood. I was especially nervous. After witnessing a performance that had as much power on drums as I'd seen thirty years earlier, I headed backstage to actually *talk* to Elvin. I was toting my memoir *Riders on the Storm* under my arm. By this time I had received many accolades about my own drumming, but what I'd just seen wasn't rock 'n' roll. It was jazz, the root of all my learning about the craft of drumming.

With trepidation, I introduced myself. My name didn't ring any bells for Elvin, so I quickly held up *Riders on the Storm* and said, "This is for you. It's my autobiography about playing in a rock band. In here I wrote that you gave me my hands."

I was prepared for condescension, jazz being the higher art, but that wasn't in Mr. Jones's repertoire. He was so incredibly kind and gracious; I was once again humbled to be in his presence. He spoke quietly as he thanked me for coming down. I felt complete. I had honored the man who had taught me so much.

Several years later, the Jazz Machine was playing the Jazz Bakery in Culver City, and I made another pilgrimage to jazz mecca. Elvin's playing hadn't deteriorated in the least. He was still channeling the pulse of the universe. After the last set, I befriended another drummer, Len Curiel, who was obviously Elvin's number-one fan. "You gotta come back and rap with him, he's very open. He'll give you his home phone number in New York. Maybe we'll all go out to eat later. I've done that with him many times."

Wow, hangin' with my mentor? "I wanna help tear down his set," I said to Len, while watching Elvin's wife unscrew a cymbal stand.

"Oh, Keiko will never let you do that," Len chuckled. "She's his manager *and* his roadie."

I spotted Dave Weckl of Chick Corea fame and Blood, Sweat, & Tears drummer Bobby Colomby, both looking up at the stage with the same idea of wanting to help, but Keiko was very protective. She had lived with her man in a two-bedroom apartment on New York's Upper West Side for forty-odd years. The neighborhood had changed, but not their dedication to each other.

Elvin's eyes lit up when I went backstage and asked him who were some of *his* mentors. "Sid Catlett, yeah, Big Sid Catlett, among many others." At the risk of looking like a fifty-year-old groupie, I asked Jones to autograph my old Coltrane LPs, which I'd brought down. "Don't be embarrassed by that," Elvin beamed as he John Hancock-ed my collector's items. I was thrilled that he put "To John" on a large poster of him that I dragged to the gig.

Keiko tried to move the party along and get the living legend home—we'd have no late-night meals with the godfather of the skins that night—but as we walked toward their car, my guru let me take the cymbal bag from under his arm and carry it the rest of the way. Though I carried Elvin Jones's bag only a few yards, it was an honor for which I'd waited thirty-five years.

Chapter Five
Jim Morrison
The Shaman

*With your feet on the ground, the
earth spirits rise up the legs.*

My third encounter with someone who seemed to have access to the other world was when I first met Jim Morrison. His direct line to the "other side" hit me quick. I was jamming at the Manzareks' garage when Ray handed me a crumpled piece of paper with Jim's lyrics to "Break on Through":

> Day destroys the night
> Night divides the day
> Tried to run, tried to hide
> Break on through to the other side

Not only were the lines rhythmic (which I, as a drummer, appreciated), but he was talking about a connection to the void, a raising of consciousness. The words were pulsing with the feelings of a Seeker, someone trying to tell us that life is bitter and sweet, but that *there is something else.*

When we first met, the term "shaman" wasn't in the cultural lexicon yet. Even though I hadn't heard of it, I read it in Jim's poems. He was well aware of the techniques of the spiritual leaders in so-called primitive tribes, how they would take psychedelic plants, get into a trance, and heal people. Jim had been a literary scholar for many years, soaking up books and poetry like a sponge. He had started writing at age fourteen and had volumes and volumes of journals chock full of his writing: poems, rants, prose. Stories spilled out of his notebooks. In later interviews, he said that his life felt like a bow being pulled back for twenty-two years and then let go.

Jim wasn't a musician per se. In fact, he couldn't play a single chord on any instrument. But as he once told me, when he heard an entire rock concert in his head and wanted to get all that sound out into the world, he thought of melodies to help him remember the lyrics (which were sheer poetry to me). What a gift. If you listen to "The Crystal Ship," for example, you'll hear the melody crossing some very sophisticated chord changes. Although Jim loved the blues, which have a simple twelve-bar form, he also hung on to some of his inner melodies with complex chord structures. Everything going on in his head was totally intuitive, and without the three of us musicians, he'd have had no form to attach it to. He could write the quintessential "Roadhouse Blues" and then the much more complicated "When the Music's Over" and still keep going. The music was never over for Jim.

Someone remarked to me that if Jim hadn't found the band, he might have died sooner. I'm still chewing on that thought. The positive side of Jim's excessiveness—his impulse to *have everything and have it now!*—channeled his angst into creativity. The negative side of it, of course, would eventually surface as substance abuse.

The late, great Tom Petty, the superb song craftsman, told me a theory of his when we were talking about Jim. "Some artists, the very very great ones, come along with the flame turned all the way up. And the flame is all the way up and you use a lot of fuel fast. And you've just got to get the heat that comes off of it." Morrison was full of creativity that had to get out one way or another. The "spirit" in the bottle eventually doused that flame. But all of us were blessed with his creative spirit for the twenty-seven years that he roamed the planet and gave us the gift of sound.

And the sound that came out of Jim's mouth was so special. At first, nerves made his voice thin, but eventually, after about a year of rehearsals, it developed into a deep baritone. Then there was his scream. It sounded like someone being crucified, a moan from the bowels of his soul. For a guy who had never sung before he met his bandmates, his voice was a huge gift from the other world. While his fellow rock singers began to have throat problems and some had to undergo surgery, Jim never seemed to hurt his pipes, even though he sometimes sounded like he had reached down into his throat and ripped it out to show the world. I guess he naturally sang from his diaphragm, which is the proper way taught by vocal coaches.

His three musical sidekicks (and it took three of us to match the energy of this one person) were lucky (and talented enough) to figure out the perfect sound bed for Jim to lie down in. When he first sang "The End" a cappella, it struck me as a goodbye love tune. But over time, as we played it in clubs, the middle section stretched out into a king-size bed for Jim to revel in. You could just feel the love and comfort he got from surrendering to the dronelike guitar, the sustained organ, and the trans groove of this song. My intuition told me to take off the snares (a typical rock sound) and play the dark and moody sound of tom-toms instead.

Jim felt safe enough, cozy in that sonic bed, to free up his subconscious mind and let out deep, dark poetic musings. He unearthed the primal, sexual, Oedipal underpinnings of all of our psyches.

The blue bus is callin' us
Driver where you takin' us?
Meet me at the back of the blue bus,
Doin' the blue rock, on a blue bus . . . yeah

Even though I didn't understand some of Jim's lyrics, I didn't question them. I felt them and they felt right. My friend Robert Bly, the American poet, once said to me that sometimes he'd write a line in one of his poems that he didn't quite understand but felt needed to be there. Wrapped in a sheet of sound, Jim exposed the archetypal undercurrents threading us all together that we normally aren't aware of. But sometimes Jim didn't seem to analyze his poetry and just let rip.

Ride the snake, to the lake, the ancient lake,
The snake he's long, seven miles, he's old
And his skin is cold, baby

We all took a chance with Jim, meeting him "at the back of the blue bus, / Doin' a blue rock," and we are forever grateful. The sound coming from the back of that bus was deep. Primal fears, primal lusts, and everything in between.

When I realized Jim was on a fast descent, I pulled back as a friend, for self-protection. Granted, as soon as we leave the cradle, we're all headed to the grave, but I knew my own descent would be more gradual. I thought what we were doing might last a decade or so, but I had no idea our lead singer was tapping into a core of universal sound vibrations, sonic waves that would reverberate for fifty years, that continue to resonate to this day.

Wynton Marsalis, who wrote *Blood on the Fields*, the first jazz composition to win the Pulitzer Prize, describes music as an "invisible force." I'm proud and grateful to have been a part of that sound with The Doors. Fueled by Jim's drive, we helped him get that concert out of his skull and into the universe. I know that "Light My Fire" was played on the Apollo 17 mission in 1972, and recently our first album was put in the Library of Congress, so the Morrison message did get out. I'm sure Jim is very happy about that.

Chapter Six

Emil Richards

Good Vibes

Music is a vibration.

O ne of the most beloved musicians who walked the planet, Emil Richards played with everybody. And I mean everybody. From Frank Sinatra to George Harrison to Ravi Shankar, his musical presence graced all the genres of sound.

My first exposure to Emil was at Shelly's Manne Hole, the jazz club in Hollywood where I saw Coltrane. I saw all the greats there, and Emil was one of them. He was playing vibes with the Paul Horn Quintet, a group that Miles said he admired. "Paul Horn plays the horn the way it should be played," the trumpet giant remarked. The alto player returned the compliment. "Miles knows how to wait. He doesn't make notes unless he has something to say. Then he speaks the truth."

The Paul Horn Quintet would do these fast jazz waltz tempos that I couldn't get enough of when I was a teenager, I'd go home and rip into my kit for hours, trying to emulate the 3/4 groove. When Emil took a solo, it was like he was buttering toast. He would lean a little to the left or right and glide those mallets over the metal vibraphone in an incredible flurry. But at the same time there seemed to be no tension in his playing. What ultimately looks easy, I found out, comes from a huge amount of work. It doesn't matter which art form you're in: painting, music, movies—they all require many hours, many years, in the woodshed.

Years after I saw Emil Richards play jazz, I went on a monthlong Maharishi meditation retreat. To my glee, Paul Horn and Emil were in attendance. At the end of the retreat, there was a jam session. Various blues and rock musicians were doing their thing when Paul and Emil went up onstage. This was my moment. With heart pounding, I too went up and said to the drummer, "I know these tunes they're gonna play." He handed me the sticks.

I started counting off one of those fast waltzes. We roared into "Fun Time," and I felt confident that what my hands were doing fit the sound—as confirmed by Emil turning around and giving me a thumbs-up! He had a big smile on his face. That moment remains with me today, fifty years later, and it still feeds me. The young drummer in his twenties was playing with two of his heroes and they approved.

Another couple of years rolled by, and George Harrison began touring with a group of very good rock musicians and Ravi Shankar, the Indian sitar master. Ravi had a small ensemble of Indian musicians with him, and Emil played with both groups. To be able to cross over into very sophisticated raga rhythms was just another example of versatility. By now we had become friends, and I relished hearing his many stories of life with the greats. "One time on the road with Frank [Sinatra], he came over to me and asked what was up with this Emil shit. . . . 'It's Emilio, isn't it!!' I said, 'Yes, Mr. Chairman!'"

The Doors' longtime recording engineer, Bruce Botnick, had gone on to record large symphony orchestras doing film music when he invited me down to a session. The infamous movie composer Jerry Goldsmith was at the helm when I walked into the control room. Bruce introduced me to the white-haired, ponytailed legend, who was friendly but had a lot on his mind. There are hundreds of musical cues to take care of when recording music for a film.

I noticed there were only about four overhead microphones out in the studio, covering what looked like eighty or ninety musicians. "Bruce, you used more mics on my drum set than you've got out there today. Wassup with that?"

"If you put them in the right places, John, it's all you need." That response reminded me of the brilliant record producer Daniel Lanois, who would mix a very echoey guitar way in the back of the sound of a record, giving the music depth and space.

I then noticed Emil Richards back with the percussionists. "Okay, I'm going to hang with my people." I looked at Goldsmith to make sure he wasn't about to record, then went into the recording room. It reminded me of playing in the high school symphony orchestra, but these weren't amateurs by any means. Emil welcomed me to the percussion section and started showing me all his stuff. He had one of the world's most diverse sets of instruments, collected from every corner of the planet.

I noticed Mike Lang at the grand piano, and he came over to kibitz. He had gone to Uni High School with me, and back then he was well on his way to becoming a great jazz pianist. All of these players were the cream of the crop of studio musicians, hired over and over to play on many recording sessions. Most of them got double and triple scale.

Jerry Goldsmith was now in the room, standing at the podium and tapping his baton on the music stand. "Cue number thirty-six please," he said to the large group of musicians. Emil motioned that it was okay for me to stay if I was very quiet. Mike Lang excused himself, saying he'd be back in a minute. Bruce's voice came over the intercom, informing the players that the tape was rolling. Jerry began conducting a complicated few minutes of full orchestral sound. When it was over, Bruce said, "That's a take!" Then Mike came back over to shoot the shit.

What blew my mind was that these players were sight-reading very complicated musical notation on the spot. I remember struggling to read music in high school. These guys were such good readers that they could do everything in one take. My respect for them was immense.

Unfortunately, the next time I saw Emil was on the DVD of the memorial for George Harrison at the Albert Hall in London. *Concert for George* was one of the most powerful tributes to a musician that anyone could hope for. The first half consisted of about fifteen of India's greatest musicians playing a composition that Ravi Shankar wrote to honor George's passing. His daughter Anoushka conducted, and Emil played marimba. He told me that Anoushka was very deliberate in her use of the baton to help the Western musicians get inside the very complicated raga melodies. It was beyond thrilling. George got a musical send-off heard by all of the angels in heaven.

Years later, having lunch with my teacher, Emil told me that he was with George just after he passed. He was at the movies with his beloved wife Celeste when George's wife Olivia called. George had already stepped off the Karmic Wheel, and Olivia invited Emil and Celeste to come over to say their goodbyes. They all performed a bedside *puja* for the Beatles' guitarist. A puja is a prayer ritual that shows reverence for a deity. Apparently, as Emil finished, he could swear he saw a smile creep over George's face.

Emil was channeling the music of the spheres. There are some spirits still walking among us that are purveyors of light. We need all the light we can get, because the darkness around us is deep. Emil was holding a flashlight into the abyss, and doing it with a smile. Twenty years ago, a doctor told him due to his smoking Camels he was going to check out soon. George Harrison had a giant percussion case made for Emil that was an exact replica of the cigarette pack.

His daughter Camille told me that one day her dad pointed to his palm and said, "See this life line . . . it's so long it goes down to my balls!" A couple years ago, at lunch, Emil said to me, "I'm going to stick around for a little while longer." I wondered how much control he had over these cosmic matters.

Now my beloved teacher has just shut off that flashlight, and I am hanging up the phone after taking the call from Celeste. She said a couple of days ago that he asked her to get into bed with him and hold him. At eighty-six, he went quick, no pain. Earlier that morning, he said to his daughter, "Today's the day!" "Oh, come on, Dad!" Camille exclaimed.

I turned the flashlight back on by playing an African drum for Emil's crossing, a drum he gave me. I dedicate the rest of my life to channeling the spark that emanated from the eyes of my fellow percussionist.

Chapter Seven

Lou Reed

Darkness Visible

If you can't see your shadow,
your Achilles' heel will grow.

t first, I didn't *get* Lou Reed.

The Velvet Underground's weeklong stand at the Whisky in 1967 was symbolic of the East Coast angst coming to sunny southern California. I didn't know that their musicianship was secondary to their message. And their message was a voice from the underground. The rage was evident as Nico, the German vamp, sang/spoke a few songs in her distinctive accent.

Václav Havel, the future Czech leader, got Lou Reed and the Velvet Underground, probably because back then he was underground himself. His plays were too politically provocative for the Czechoslovakian government, so they threw him in jail. Lou Reed's music fed Havel's psyche and inspired him to work to become president of the Czech Republic. The nonviolent revolution in the Czech Republic was named after Lou's band—the Velvet Revolution. Back in this country, right-wing fundamentalists who broke rock 'n' roll records on the air for being the "devil's music" didn't realize that the music had become the best ad for democracy that America would ever have.

Our lead singer certainly got Nico . . . literally. A few years later, I was rooming next door to Jim at the Great Northern Hotel in Manhattan, and he and Nico kept me up all night with their antics. There was a lot of crashing around, which worried me, but they looked okay in the morning. Later, in the press, Nico said, "Ja, Jim ist crazy!"

I knew I was drumming for some dark lyrics ("mother, father . . . I want to!!"), and I should have realized that the Velvets were exploring the same terrain. Like Jim, Lou saw no reason not to put gritty, literate lyrics on top of rock 'n' roll.

My next encounter with the man from Brooklyn was on the set of a tongue-in-cheek parody film on rock 'n' roll called *Get Crazy*. I was cast as a heavy-metal rock drummer, and Lou got to emulate the cover of Bob Dylan's *Bringing It All Back Home*. That was one of the very few cool moments in the movie.

Lou, who was still coming out of heavy drug use, was sweating as he climbed the stairs to the set. I was coming down and said, "Lou, John Densmore. You're one of the reasons I accepted this role. 'Waves of Fear' is a really good song." He looked at me like I was crazy. I think he was shocked that I had appreciated one of his more obscure songs. He looked like he was experiencing the subject of that song: withdrawal.

After his "walk on the wild side," Mr. Reed cleaned up his act and made some great solo albums, which spanned several decades. I still can't get enough of his 1989 album *New York*, which tackles almost every issue possible, from AIDS to pollution to crime to the pope to the whales. For any other songwriter, covering all these bases could be risky, even corny, but with Lou at the wheel, it was magnificent.

The next time our paths crossed was at a book fair in New York. Lou had just come back from the Czech Republic. President Havel had summoned the rocker to come and do an interview. It was a thank-you gesture from the former renegade writer, who had found solace in the rocker's music when he was down and out. Lou was visibly excited to tell me about the experience. He also seemed very together physically, which was a relief. By surviving, he was feeding the rest of us gifts of art.

Since Lou wanted his music to be programmatic with the gritty lyrics, he used his guitar like a gun, pelting the listener with a spray of sonic bullets. "I'm very emotionally affected by sound," said the Velvet's lead singer. He tuned all his strings to one note and coined the term "Ostrich guitar" to describe the sound. Then he would whack the strings with his strumming hand, percussively slapping all our faces. He wanted to wake people up. He knew *exactly* what he was doing. "Sound is inexplicable, like light," Lou rhapsodized. "Ordered sound is music."

Like the entire city of New York, I was devastated by Reed's passing. His wife Laurie Anderson wrote such a heartfelt goodbye in *Rolling Stone* that I'm sure no one could read it without their tear ducts opening up. Mine flooded. She had held Lou in her arms as he passed. At the very end, he had seemed ready. The sometimes tortured soul was finally calm.

Like Jim Morrison, Lou Reed constantly questioned the boundaries of human nature. In a 1987 *Rolling Stone* interview with David Fricke, Lou said, quoting Bette Davis in *All about Eve*, "I hate cheap sentiment." Well, at the risk of cheap sentimentality, thanks, Lou, for being my man (feeding me so much musical dope, as in "I'm Waiting for the Man"), and thanks, Laurie, for your loving tribute to your man. I give back to you a line about death from the poet Galway Kinnell: "The wages of dying is love."

Chapter Eight

Janis Joplin

Abandon

Let it rip! And it will rip.

I realized I was once again in the presence of someone gifted when I met Janis Joplin, who ultimately turned into a music icon for the world, and we are all the better for it. Sadly, Janis's psychic wounds took her down before she could ever really take that in.

The mellow Chet Helms, who eventually ran the Avalon, the "other" ballroom in San Francisco, lived the dream with Janis. Back in Texas, the young Joplin had been busy feeding her muse by tacking up all her feelings on the garage wall via newspaper and magazine photos and being one of the very first of her gender to wear "boys' clothes," jeans and Levi jackets, although the cowboy ethic drove her out of Texas. She hitchhiked across the country to San Francisco because Chet, who knew her in Texas, needed a lead singer for the band he man-aged. They both found a home in the Bay Area.

The psychedelic ballrooms in San Francisco were an ex-treme departure from the concept of ballroom dancing. The visionary promoter Bill Graham would forever change the way rock 'n' roll was presented. He had the courage to book three acts a night from extremely different genres—rock, jazz, and blues. The racial mix was totally diverse as well. In one night you might see Sly and the Family Stone, the Grateful Dead, and a bluegrass group while the walls pulsed with "light shows."

On our third sojourn up to the city by the bay, The Doors were on the marquee at Graham's Fillmore Auditorium with Jefferson Airplane and the James Cotton Blues Band. After we finished our first set at the Fillmore, Airplane's bass player, Jack Cassidy, came over to Robby and me.

"Hey, you guys should go over to the Avalon and see Big Brother and the Holding Company," he said.

Big Brother? *What kinda name is that for a band?* I thought to myself. *Are they Nazi sympathizers?* Plus, it would be really tight getting back in time for our second set.

"You've got at least an hour and a half with us and James Cotton playing sets," Cassidy said. "You *really* should see the singer."

At his insistence, Robby and I got in our rental car and jammed over to Van Ness Avenue from Fillmore Street. Walk-ing up the white steps and into the large white room (the colored-light shows were projected against white sheets draped over all the walls and the ceiling), we could hear a raw bluesy sound coming from the stage.

The female vocalist was singing with such conviction (and desperation) that I was transfixed. We worked our way up to the side of the stage, where we watched her move, between the chorus ("Down on me, down on me") and the verses, as if possessed. The soul of some ancient blues singer seemed to have shot up in an electric current from the floor and ignited her body. She was wrestling with the mic stand, choking it and pulling it back and forth like it was someone she had in a stranglehold. Her passion was intense. It made me think that I should inject more of what she had into my drumming. Damn, that woman had soul.

They finished their set, and I went back to meet this incredible young singer. Her name was Janis Joplin.

After giving everything one could possibly give onstage, Janis was cooling off with shots from her gallon jug of Red Mountain wine, real rotgut. She gave me a very warm and friendly smile, offering me a slug. I took a hit and gave it back, telling her I loved what she was doing but had to rush back to the Fillmore for our last set. I knew Robby and I had just seen someone we would be hearing from again . . . and again. There was no doubt where she was going—straight up the charts.

She put a spell on the listener. The one time I saw Aretha live, I thought, *This woman can rile up an entire audience on one note!* Janis dreamed of having that kind of ability. She said, "Billie Holiday, Aretha Franklin . . . they are so subtle, they can milk you with two notes, they can go no farther than A to B, and they can make you feel like they told you the whole universe. . . . I don't know that yet, all I got now is strength, but maybe if I keep singing, maybe I'll get it." Back then, I put

Janis in the same category, even if she thought she hadn't made it yet.

The next time I caught up with Janis was many, many years later at Woodstock. She was a huge superstar now, having practically stolen the whole show at the Monterey Pop Festival with her performance of "Ball and Chain." The audience was just staring at the young white singer, mouths gaping open, like Mama Cass, who was in the front row. Ms. Joplin had an entourage now and wasn't as warm and friendly as she'd been back at the Avalon. The change in her may also have come from the monkey she had on her back now: drugs.

At a party in Los Angeles around the time Jim was well on his way to becoming an alcoholic, he pulled on Janis's hair and she responded by cracking a bottle of Southern Comfort over his head. Just a couple of drunks, headed for the gutter. But they couldn't help themselves. Living life with total abandon was their mantra. As Janis sang in "Piece of My Heart," she knew no boundaries and literally gave away too much. "I make love to twenty-five thousand people at a concert, then go home alone."

I'm reminded of a dream Jim told me he had: "We do a big concert, then go back to the hotel, and while walking down the hallway to my room, I hear voices. As I get closer, I wonder if I'm on the wrong floor or something. I check my key, and sure enough, it's my room, but a big party is going on in there. I slowly open the door and a bunch of people glance at me as if they don't know me, then go on partying."

Not all artists are cursed with creativity and self-destruction in the same package, but these two were. After Woodstock, the Hippie Dream got stuck in a bottle or in a vein. It would take a resurgence of the ideals of Alcoholics Anonymous to get the dream of being "happy, joyous, and free" back into the light.

Dave Hayward, Janis's trumpet player, tells the story of what happened once when they were headed from New York to Nashville for a gig. Joplin felt that she needed to woo the country audience, and so she picked Kris Kristofferson's "Me and Bobby McGee" as a song to cover. A choice so perfect, it not only wooed the country crowd, the recording of the song became her only number-one single. Her performance put the listener right inside the cab of that truck she was singin' about, singin' songs of freedom. "Me and Bobby McGee" became the second posthumous number-one single in US chart history, after "(Sittin' on) the Dock of the Bay" by Otis Redding.

Unfortunately, Janis's substance abuse caught up with her, and she didn't get to see the huge success produced by her last album, *Pearl*. In the words of one of the great songwriters, Randy Newman, "It's Lonely at the Top." Knowing that made me less jealous of the center spotlight onstage. I was in the back, and maybe that was a safer place to be. Back there you could get singed a little from the attention, but you were breathing in less of the helium going straight upstairs to the ego.

Janis and Jim were two of those great center-stage artists whose demons caught up with them. Two cautionary tales indeed. You don't have to be self-destructive and burn out to be creative, but some artists simply can't help it. Jimi Hendrix had a bright, creative future ahead of him and just made a mistake mixing substances, but Joplin and Morrison were channeling Apollo *and* Dionysus at the same time.

It doesn't have to be that way; many great artists live to a ripe old age, continuing to create right up to the end. But when you're not only gifted but tortured, after a time the human family seems more fascinated with your troubles than your art. It's kinda sad. It's as if we are jealous of someone with creative gifts, and when they fall, we revel in them having to pay for being so special. Randy Newman is right: the air is thin up there.

I've had relationship struggles, including several divorces, but I've never regretted any of those unions. They ran their course and ultimately led to another very deep union with someone else. Janis never found the right companion to go with her and help her as she made her unique human journey. But she certainly gave us the companionship of her incredible creations. The recordings of her astonishing pipes fill us up with the warmth of being human. I sure hope, wherever Janis is, she can feel our love and now take in the appreciation of the gifts she gave us.

Chapter Nine

Ray Manzarek

Improvisation

Life is one big improv.

A slew of books on The Doors have been published—including not one but two memoirs of my own—but none of them have focused on that bespectacled organ wizard Ray Manzarek. You see, Ray came with two musicians inside his one frame. Let's go back to the beginning.

After meeting Ray at the Maharishi meditation class in 1965, I ventured down to his parents' Manhattan Beach house to attend a jam session. I drove up the alley where I heard rock 'n' roll coming from the garage. Ray came out of the front house, walking down the narrow passageway between these beach cottages. He wore a blue long-sleeved dress shirt with the sleeves rolled up and the top unbuttoned halfway. His white pants were also rolled up to reveal flip-flops on his feet. In a buttonhole of his shirt he had placed a daisy.

Ray broke into the warmest smile as he directed me where to park. He certainly looked more relaxed than at the meditation class the previous night. That had been a follow-up meeting after we were all initiated, and Ray was complaining about not getting the instant "bliss" that was promised, he thought, by Jerry Jarvis, the instructor. I knew meditation wasn't going to have effects as instant as LSD, so I was willing to try it for a while and see how it went.

Ray and I broke the ice when we started talking about our mutual love of jazz. I told him that I had seen all the greats at the Manne Hole in Hollywood: Miles, Coltrane, Art Blakey, Cannonball Adderley, Bill Evans, and so on.

"Bill Evans!" Ray exclaimed. He was jealous.

"His genius is in his touch," I waxed.

"Yeah," Ray agreed, adding, "Miles got crap for having this mellow white guy in the band, but he knew how good he was."

"Yeah, man. Miles doesn't take shit from anybody! Do you know *All Blues*?" I prompted.

"Let's do it!" Ray said enthusiastically.

Now we would break the musical ice. The tune is in 3/4 time, a waltz tempo that is a good test of whether a musician can "swing." Ray and I locked immediately. That felt good.

A major component of jazz is improvisation, which forces you to stay in the moment because you never know what will be coming up. There's a lot of freedom and space available as you improvise around the chord changes. In jazz improvisation or in a rock guitar solo, mere speed doesn't guarantee the most creative solo (thank God). It's a balance between sound and space, between lyricism and virtuosity. It's about breathing in and breathing out. Sometimes it's cool to show your shit (demonstrating how fast you can play), but when it comes organically out of an entire solo, it's better. Kinda like being human: sometimes we have to run, sometimes we get to chill.

You can read about what happened after that jam session in all those other Doors books. The extremely important thing to know is that Ray was the first to see the magic in Jim Morrison. He even received flak from some of his fellow UCLA film students for hanging out with Jim. They thought Jim was too crazy. The first set of lyrics Ray gave me—I think intentionally—was for "Break on Through (to the Other Side)." He had immediately resonated with Jim's connection to the world behind this world—or, to quote Michael Meade again, "the world where this world came from"—just as I did.

Another extremely important musical moment happened a month later. We had been auditioning bass players and didn't seem to be getting anywhere. Ray said that he'd seen a Fender electric keyboard bass he wanted to try. I went with him to Glenn Wallichs's Music City in Hollywood to check it out. After parking, we passed the display window of the musical instrument department, and there it was, sitting on top of a stand. It looked like a couple of octaves (twenty-four black-and-white keys) with a silver chrome top.

"Let's go through the record department quickly," I said, "because if we look at all, we'll never get to the instrument department."

Ray knew what I meant. Years before, I got stuck listening for hours in the record booths. What a great store! You could actually play something before you bought it. Started by Glenn Wallichs and songsmith Johnny Mercer, Music City was mecca for all southern California music junkies. "I drooled over all of Coltrane's LPs in that booth," I said as we passed the brown mahogany listening section and entered the musical instruments department.

Ray asked if he could play the keyboard bass, and the rep plugged it into an amp. Ray began doing those repetitive lines he was experimenting with on our new songs. "I'm thinking of playing this with my left hand and the organ with my right."

"It sounds like it has enough punch," I said. We didn't want the bass to sound mushy, which could have been a trap without a separate bass player plucking a string. (Remember, this was before the advent of synthesizers and computers, which eventually could duplicate almost any sound in the world.)

The keyboard bass was a few hundred bucks, significant money then, but we bought it. This was a pivotal moment in the formation of our sound. It forced Ray to play the keys more sparsely with his right hand only, and it also made him simplify his left-hand bass lines.

Now in rehearsals I concentrated on connecting with Ray's left hand. Bass players and drummers are like brothers, working in the basement, cooking up the groove. If they don't lock together with the feel, the ensemble will suck. You can have a brilliant drummer and bass player and a lousy guitarist and the band will survive, but if the rhythm section (bass and drums) is lousy, it won't fly, no matter how brilliant the guitarist is.

You see, for drummers one beat is extremely long. Let me quote my second memoir (*The Doors: Unhinged*):

The space between one beat and the next is extremely important, since the space implies the feel of the entire composition. If you play on the front of the beat, as in military music, Irish music, polkas, etc. (the style I learned in my high school marching band), the feel is rather controlled. I used this style way back when I played bar mitzvahs. On the other hand, if you perform with the accent on the back of the beat (if you don't hit the next beat until the last second), the feel is very laid-back as in the blues, R&B, ballads, etc. I certainly got this style down from performing for years in bars.

When The Doors got started, we covered the blues a lot until we had enough originals, so our foundation was first built on a laid-back feel. If you wait until the last mini-second to come in with the second beat, you're playing the blues . . . leaving as much room as possible for the "sadness" to enter. Then the originals, with Jim's percussive lyrics, pushed the pulse forward a little. Thank God Ray and I were in the same arena when we wrote the music to these words.

Simply put, if Ray and I had not felt the pulse for Jim's lyrics the same way, there would have been no Doors. I don't mean to be self-congratulatory here. What I do mean to stress is that the rhythm section is the foundation of any ensemble, whether it's a quartet or a forty-piece orchestra, and without a strong foundation, the structure will crumble.

It eventually turned out that with Ray and me as that foundation, Robby could build the walls for Jim to sit on top of as the roof . . . or up front as the lead singer. The walls were formidable because of Robby's gifted songwriting skills. If there is mutual respect, the structure will have balance and be very solid. So I credit the pairing of Ray's left hand and my drumming as a blessing from the muse.

Now let's talk about Ray splitting his brain in two. He simultaneously had to lock into a repetitive bass pulse with his left hand and support Jim's lyrics playing chord changes with his right. To do this, he said, he thought of playing boogie-woogie bass lines that he learned as a kid in Chicago. If that wasn't enough, he occasionally came up with the most memorable keyboard hooks (musical segues) in popular music.

Think of the intro to "Light My Fire." It's a circle of fifths, played in a baroque (Bach-like) style. This keyboard part is permanently stamped on everyone's brain. We will never forget it. Or take what he created in "Riders on the Storm," the mysterious sound supporting Jim's dark lyrics. It was an incredible extended piano solo that I rode with him up and down the full arc of human emotions. From pianissimo to fortissimo and everything in between, that solo of Ray's will also be stamped on all our brains forever.

You only need to hear a couple of bars of music from a great artist and you can identify who it is. Elvin Jones, Ravi Shankar, Janis Joplin, Bob Marley, Van and Jim Morrison . . . practically every chapter of this book is about someone whose work is instantly recognizable. Read a couple of sentences of Joseph Campbell and you know it's him. You hear Ray's hand on a Vox organ and you know who it is in three seconds.

Maybe it's sadness over losing Ray—my early father figure has crossed over—but these days I aspire to having an even better relationship with my old keyboard player than before. I make a joke about this over and over concerning my deceased mother, but maybe it's not really a joke. An even bigger space can open up in the wake of a significant person's departure. My mind tends to go to my mother and to Ray more often now, because I know that I can't reach them on a physical level. As Maharishi said before he passed, "I will be available anywhere, instantly!"

For instance, having dinner in a French restaurant, I flip my fork over like Europeans do and immediately think of Ray. He and his wife Dorothy always ate that way, looking like sophisticated continental diners. As a twenty-year-old, I was intimidated by their sophistication. I felt clumsy with my less refined manners.

My self-esteem did get a lift when we toured France, where my pidgin French served me well while Ray and Dorothy retreated into silence. When I was young, I aspired to be like the extremely cultured ivory tinkler in our band, and I'm still working on it. Back then, Ray was exceptionally well read, and now I'm catching up. He is still my teacher, now more than ever. I've recently had some medical issues around my abdomen (burst appendix), the same area of the body that took Ray out. My compassion for him has increased twofold now that my own experience has made me more aware of how he must have suffered.

Okay, I'm sure some of you readers right now are thinking: it's sweet that John is talking to the dead (Ray), but let's get real—there's no actual communication once people you knew "Break on Through to the Other Side." All I can say is, it's more than just mental candy, this expectation that I'm going to jam again with Ray in that big band in the sky. Musicians are serious when they talk about all the incredible musicians now playing in God's orchestra. There's a very deep bond between "melody makers."

Check out Ray's masterful solo album *Golden Scarab* to see clearly into his metaphysical side. "The idea that the soul will join with the ecstatic just because the body is rotten—that is all fantasy. What is found now is found then. If you find nothing now, you will simply end up with an apartment in the City of Death. If you make love with the divine now, in the next life you will have the face of satisfied desire." So said the great Indian poet Kabir.

Or as George Harrison put it in speaking of his connection to John Lennon: "We saw beyond each other's physical bodies. If you can't feel the spirit of some friend who's been that close, then what chance have you got of feeling the spirit of Christ or Buddha or whoever else you may be interested in?" So I'm coming out of the closet right now and admitting that I've had several conversations with George since he passed, and I'm surely going to keep talking with Ray. I talk to Jim all the time.

I'm starting to worry that I now sound like my devoted Catholic mother, who is "gonna see all her friends in Heaven." I don't *see* things quite that literally. I feel that when the body passes, the spirit continues, but in what form that energy manifests I haven't a clue. It's a mystery to me . . . a great mystery. That's why when asked if I believe in God, I answer, "I believe in the Mystery, with a capital M."

Maybe that's why Ray had a giant art deco poster with a big "M" in the middle. Of course, the "M" stood for Manzarek, which implies he had a large ego. When I challenged Ray in my first memoir that he might be working the Willy Loman beat a little too hard (the selling of The Doors), he got back at me by saying in his own book that Jim had hated me "as a human being." Jim might very well have said that, probably while tripping, and maybe because I didn't do as many drugs as he did. But you see, Jim and I are okay with that now. I sacrificed over five years of my life trying to preserve Jim's legacy through a brutal court battle. It's amusing (or prophetic) how in *Riders* I used what I thought was just a technique to communicate with Jim: writing him a continuing letter in the first person, as if he could hear me even though he had passed. Now I feel the love energy not only with Jim but with Ray too.

Toward the end of our career, a philosophical gap grew between Ray and me. You can read all about it in *The Doors: Unhinged*, but here it suffices to say that I was so angry at him I felt it would take several incarnations to forgive him. Writing *Unhinged* helped. As I wrote in the last chapter of that book, how could I not love Ray? We had created magic together in a garage, so many years ago. I sent that last chapter to Ray and Robby before the book was published, to make sure they got to that section, because the first half was going to be a tough pill for them to swallow.

Even amid those philosophical and personal struggles, the two of us never lost the almost telepathic communication we had on the musical level. Ray understood the avant-garde, and he understood dark matter. He was comfortable, as I was, with venturing outside traditional rhythmic and chord structures, but he also knew that eventually you had to get back or you would leave the cosmos and your audience behind.

When to come back is the question, and that is one that can only be answered intuitively. The astrophysicist Neil deGrasse Tyson says that the earth doesn't just rotate around the sun, that it is also affected by the gravitational pull of *all* the planets in our solar system. A musical ensemble is the same. The rhythm section (Ray's left hand and me) vibrates at a lower frequency, supporting the lead players. All of the celestial bodies in our solar system push and pull each other, to varying degrees, while the sun is the lead singer.

Balance is everything. If the ice caps are melting, or if the guitar player is too loud, life gets out of balance (*koyaanisqatsi*). That's why the really accomplished musicians listen *intently* to their fellow players. They put aside their egos. If one of the musicians gets a little too full of himself when he's the focal point, the "star," the surrounding planets have to adjust. But sometimes the star spins out of orbit and no amount of adjusting will bring him back.

Ray and I were completely in sync when it came to finding common musical ground. The musical background each of us brought to our partnership fed us well and fertilized our unique feel and sound. With my drums and Ray's left hand as the bottom, Robby Krieger's liquid guitar completed the sound. The resulting melting pot was an American gumbo that Jim obviously couldn't get enough of. I say that not out of arrogance. Just think about it: here was a guy who had never sung before and who, after getting over his shyness, sang from the bowels of his vocal chords. He was in heaven lying on the bed of sound we made for him. Without Manzarek, our quartet would have sounded like a three-legged dog.

When I heard that Ray was getting really sick, I gave him a call. Our relationship had obviously been strained, so I was very pleased that he picked up the phone. We talked about his bout with cancer, and I said to give his wife Dorothy my love. At the time I didn't know it was going to be my last conversation with him. I'm so grateful that we had a closing talk.

I will forever miss this remarkable, gifted musician. After Ray passed, I called Robby, told him death trumps everything, suggested we get together. We recently played some Doors songs at a film screening at the Los Angeles County Art Museum. It felt so good. After only a few bars, we were back in the garage in Venice, California. Music is a healing salve.

Chapter Ten
Van Morrison
"The Flow"

If I ventured in the slipstream,
Between the viaducts of your dreams . . .

O n the night The Doors were fired from our first
club gig, Ronnie Harran, the booker for the famous
Whisky a Go Go, saw us and offered us the "house
band" slot up the street. The London Fog Club had dumped
us not because Jim was in a fog that night (which he sometimes
was), but because a fight broke out and they blamed the band.
Fortunately, Ronnie had good ears and knew we were headed
somewhere. She also headed with the handsome lead singer to
her boudoir, but that's another story.

The first set at the Whisky was at 9:00 p.m., when nobody
was in the club. The headliner came next, then we did our second set, and finally the headliner closed the night.

We were quite nervous those first few weeks. The result was a *horrible* review from Pete Johnson of the *LA Times*. It was so horrible that, as I told the rest of the band, maybe it was *good* negative PR, since it made us sound like something interesting to see. After getting our feet wet, we jumped in full throttle and tried to blow off the stage each of the famous acts that had the big billing. The Rascals, Paul Butterfield, The Turtles, The Seeds, Frank Zappa and the Mothers of Invention, The Animals, The Beau Brummels, Buffalo Springfield, Captain Beefheart—all of them had to deal with us. I mean, of course we loved and admired all of these creative musicians, but we also were a force to be reckoned with ourselves.

We started to develop a following, freaks who loved free-form dancing and would show up for our first set each night. The great owner-promoter Elmer Valentine smartly took down the go-go dancing cages, sensing the new movement of "hippies" forming. It was our turf now. After we finished some of our songs, instead of applause, silence filled the room.

Most people are afraid of silence. We weren't. The astrophysicist Tyson says that "dark matter"—the spaces in between the stars and the planets—is as important as matter, and perhaps even more important. Likewise, it's the space the musician makes in between the notes that gives music the human element. When drum machines were first invented many years ago, they had a "human" button, which, when pressed, sped up or slowed down the machine. I guess human error is a good thing, or at least something that elicits compassion. So something scary, but very attractive to humans, resides in that "dark matter" space where sound gets swallowed up by silence. Complete emptiness. The Void. It was hard for some acts to follow us because of the ominous vibe we left in the air.

We heard that Elmer booked Them, the Irish band whose lead singer, Van Morrison, had penned "Gloria" and "Mystic Eyes" and so compellingly adapted "Baby, Please Don't Go" to suit his voice and band. We were in awe. As the date approached, the decision to take our cover version of "Gloria" out of our set seemed wise. We thought our take of the song was pretty good, but it was not cool to step on the originator's toes.

On opening night for the "boys from Belfast," The Doors started with a nervous first set. During intermission, I situated myself at my usual spot on the stairway to the upper balcony. My first book, *Riders on the Storm*, sets the tone:

> Them brashly took the stage. They slammed through several songs one right after another, making them indistinguishable. Van seemed drunk and very uptight, crashing the mike stand down on the stage. But when he dropped his lower jaw and tongue and let out one of those yells of rage, something Irish in me made my skin crawl with goose bumps. Ancient angst.

I was confused about this singer having so much talent while being so self-conscious. Ronnie drove me, Van, and a few other people to a small party at her apartment at 2:00 a.m. Most of us made small talk, while Van glowered in the corner. Then all of a sudden he grabbed Ronnie's guitar and blasted into vocals, singing about being a stranger in this world and wanting to be reincarnated into another time with another face. Ultimately, these lyrics would end up on the transcendental *Astral Weeks* album. *Riders* tells what happened next:

> It was as if Van couldn't communicate on a small-talk party level, so he just burst into his songs. We were mesmerized.

It didn't seem appropriate to shower him with compliments, because his music came from such a deep place. So when he finished there was silence for a minute or so. A sacred silence.

I had been somewhat aware of the quiet in between the sounds way back in the sixties. Back then, I hadn't figured out the importance of both silence and sound in music. I had only an intuitive understanding of it. Once we started getting to know the Irish lads during that magical week, The Doors put "Gloria" back into our set list. The very last night before Van and his crew went back to the Old Sod we all played "Gloria" together. Two drummers, two keyboards, two of everything. Even two Morrisons. After about twenty minutes, we all put "Gloria" to bed after a glorious night.

Van went on to pen many, many important songs. "Brown Eyed Girl, "Crazy Love," and "Moondance," to name just a few. With "Into the Mystic," he seemed to be pointed in a more spiritual direction, which culminated with the hypnotic *Astral Weeks*. Using jazz musicians and not rehearsing beforehand, *Astral Weeks* is an impressionistic stream of consciousness. It remains a cult favorite to this day, despite the fact that it failed to achieve significant mainstream sales success for decades. After thirty-three years, it finally achieved gold in 2001. I've always said that *Astral Weeks* is one of my all-time favorite albums, and that sentiment seems widely shared, considering how many lists of "Greatest Albums of All Time" include it.

On November 6, 2008, I got a phone call from "Van's people," inquiring whether I wanted to play "Gloria" with him and his band at the Hollywood Bowl. "The Man" would perform some of his oldies up to intermission, then the brilliant album *Astral Weeks* in the second half. Hell yes! After all, I'd already played "Gloria" with him, his band, and my band at the Whisky in 1966.

I went to the afternoon rehearsal for "Gloria" at the Bowl. There were about fifteen musicians onstage, which is an unusually large group. I guessed that, for the second half, Van needed extra players, strings and the like, to replicate the sound of *Astral Weeks*. Bobby Ruggiero waved his hand for me to sit down on his drum stool. I did so, then looked out at the thousands of empty seats. Having played this venue twice, I was comfortable sitting on the drum riser and excited about the night that lay ahead. I tested out each drum. It felt easy, which was a relief. With drum sets, the angles are all different for each player, and playing on your own kit feels like wearing a comfortable glove.

Van was nowhere in sight, but they wanted to rehearse. We jumped into the song, and the backup singers sang Van's lead parts. It was a groove kicking this big band on a tune I knew very well. I threw in my own signature licks, and the musicians turned around, acknowledging me with big smiles.

Then they stopped and said, "We might do a Bo Diddley section in the middle."

"Okay," I responded. "I should know that ahead of time."

"Well, it's up to Van."

"Okay. Where is he?"

"In the dressing room."

"Okay. Why don't we ask him?"

I could feel a very pregnant pause, and then tension mounting among the players. No one was getting up to go ask Van about the arrangement. It was awkward, because if I didn't know how they were going to play that section, I could fuck it up and that would be embarrassing for all concerned. I had heard horror stories about Van, like the time he screamed at one of his roadies for bringing him the wrong vintage of wine, but I had a long history with the guy, so I wasn't going to let that deter me.

"Okay, fine! I'll ask him!" I said getting up from the drum stool. The musicians looked at me with amazement as I headed toward the dressing rooms. They seemed to actually be afraid of their lead vocalist.

I put my ear up to one of the dressing room doors and could hear Van on the phone. I rapped. He didn't respond. I rapped harder. Nothing. Then I banged hard, and he finally responded. "Yeah, what?"

"Van, it's John Densmore. Are you going to do the Bo Diddley section in the middle of 'Gloria?'"

"Whatever you want" was his response, as he went back to his conversation.

We finished rehearsing, and I went home. When I came back in the evening with my girlfriend Ildiko, we went backstage, since Van had already started. His manager told me the plan was for "Gloria" to be the encore just before intermission. I would walk out with Van, he would introduce me, and then we'd play the song. Easy enough.

Ildiko and I listened to several songs from the side of the stage. They sounded good, although up close, it was clear that Van wasn't relaxed. Something inside him seemed to be always on pins and needles.

They finished the last song, and Van the Man exited stage right. Later, Ildiko would say that she could feel Van's nervous energy. I stood beside him as we waited for our cue. He asked about Ray and Robby, which was sweet. I was reminded of that time a few months after he finished the Whisky gig years ago when I saw him in town and he asked, "How's Jim doing?" Two Morrisons caring about each other.

We walked out together on that magnificent stage under the shell at the Hollywood Bowl, but I could tell that Van couldn't take in the applause he was getting. Something was torturing him. Then he began to torture me, though not on purpose, I think. In his preoccupied state of mind, he forgot to introduce me. The band was waiting for their cue to start the song, and it didn't come. The awkward silence needed to be broken, so the guitar player started the opening chords to "Gloria." After a few bars, the rest of the band had to kick in, so they did.

Leaving me standing there in front of ten thousand people, wondering what to do. Walking off would have been weird. I spotted a tambourine under the backup singers' riser, so I walked over, picked it up, and started playing it as if that had been part of the plan. Needless to say, *I was not happy*. At that moment, I didn't give a shit about how talented Van was. This was humiliating.

No one in the audience knew that anything was wrong, but yours truly felt tremendously awkward as I worked my way over to Bobby, the drummer. We were trying to figure out how to switch—him jumping up and grabbing the tambourine, me grabbing his sticks and sitting down without missing a beat. It couldn't be done. If we tried it, the beat would definitely drop for a few bars, and Van the Man would have definitely been pulled out of his "flow." He would have turned around with a big frown on his face, even though he himself had caused the problem. So I just continued to play the tambourine with a fake smile.

At the finish, we all headed for the wings, with the roaring crowd fading as we exited. Van seemed to disappear. His manager came up to me expounding major apologies. No one would dare try to go look for "The Man" to get his take, let alone an apology.

Ildiko gave me a big hug when I met her at our box seats for the second half. Only she and the Doors' manager, Jeff Jampol, knew what I had been through. After a few songs from one of my favorite albums of all time, *Astral Weeks*, we left. The performance wasn't bad, but the vibe, which only Jeff, me, and our two girlfriends knew about, had taken the wind out of our Van Morrison sails.

Since then, I've reduced the capital letter "M" to lowercase "m" when I write about him: Van the man. Also, this book is subtitled *Meetings with Remarkable Musicians*, not *Meetings with Remarkable Men*, for a reason. Van blew it. I was going to pay him a compliment in front of ten thousand people, but he didn't remember to introduce me, so he didn't get that compliment. I was going to say, "It's a great honor to be playing with a Morrison again."

It took me a year or so to get over what had happened because, when someone you know behaves badly, it can cloud your appreciation of their work. Anytime one of Van's songs came on the radio, I had to change the station. Later, admiration for his gifts crept back into my psyche. "Into the Mystic" won me over again. I just can't resist the spiritually brilliant music The Man has produced.

When Van Morrison sings, "We were born before the wind, / Also younger than the sun," he is talking about "the flow." Even with all his phobias, he usually taps into the jet stream of sound circling the planet. Van has described that feeling in interviews: "It's just plugging in and going with the flow and then sourcing that energy."

Jay-Z speaks of getting into "the flow" while rapping. It's the rapper's choice whether to go fast with an amazing cadence, like Eminem, or wonderfully slow, like Snoop Dogg. It's how the rap sits on top of the beats, just as it's a drummer's choice whether to push the feel or to lay back. Singers make choices through their phrasing, deciding when to start a line and how long to drag it out.

Van, who obviously listened to early R&B, is impeccable when he's into his flow. Randy Lewis, the esteemed music critic for the *LA Times*, hit the nail on the head: "Van Morrison strives to reach a special space through music, an ethereal place perhaps best summarized in the title of his 1970 song 'Into the Mystic.' 'Just like way back in the days of old, [and] magnificently we will float into the mystic.'"

Chapter Eleven

Ravi Shankar
The Trance

To get high . . . breathe deep.

George Harrison called him "the Godfather of World Music," and the title fits. Ravi Shankar almost single-handedly turned the West on to the music of the East.

In the 1930s, Ravi Shankar came over to the West as a youth with his brother Uday's dance troupe. They hung out with Paramahansa Yogananda, one of the first Indian gurus to open our third eye to the spirituality that has been going on in Gandhiji's country for thousands and thousands of years. Yogananda came to the United States in the 1950s as part of the first Hindu wave, and some of Gandhi's ashes are enshrined at Yogananda's West Los Angeles meditation grounds. So early on Mr. Shankar had his creative impulses dipped in spiritual curry sauce of the highest caliber.

My first exposure to the trancelike ragas was at Ray Manzarek's apartment in Venice, California. Paul Ferrera, a friend of both Ray and Jim, had just done the artwork for one of Ravi's LPs, which lay on the wood floor along with several others in Ray's LP collection. We sat around smoking herb and listening to the master of the sitar. Actually, we didn't need the help of ganja, because the vibe coming from the East via music was instant meditation. It had an immediately calming effect . . . that is, until the climax at the end of the ten- to fifteen-minute pieces.

Ravi explained that the West needed to learn to be a little more patient. If one waits a long time for the excitement to come, it pays off big when it does. Sort of like a giant orgasm, but that's my Western libido speaking. Ravi was speaking of a spiritual payoff, after years of discipline learning the instrument and surrendering to the long intros in raga music. Music played in the Eastern tradition of modalism (phrases repeated over and over) affects the nervous system, creating a certain psychological state.

If the universe is composed of sonic vibrations, music can help you understand the world and your place in it. Haki Madhubuti, the esteemed poet and founder of Third World Press, says that "a thousand kinds of music play every hour, if we become awake enough to orchestrate our own inner resonance." Ray also turned me on to the soundtrack of Satyagit Ray's film *Pather Panchali*, a beautiful fusion of Indian music and jazz, two musical styles that rely heavily on improvisation. Shankar scored the music for the film.

Many years later, Robby Krieger and I enrolled in Ravi Shankar's Kinnara School of Music in Los Angeles. Studying the sitar and tabla (Indian drums), respectively, we were in awe of the discipline and atmosphere at the school on Fairfax Avenue at Pico Boulevard. In the classical Indian tradition, drummers have to learn to sing the notes before playing them—*tita-gita-tita-nana, tita-gita-tita-da*. The tabla is definitely the most difficult percussion instrument in the world. We crammed in a couple of months of lessons in between tours with The Doors.

Across the pond, the Beatles were following the same track, especially George Harrison. This was back in a time before social media, via the internet, so everybody didn't know what everybody else was doing. Therefore Carl Jung must have been right about synchronicity and archetypal undercurrents. The Fab Four, like the four Doors, were experimenting with then-legal LSD, and they later drifted toward meditation. It is rumored that John Coltrane was imbibing lysergic acid before recording the album *Meditations*. It's not an uncommon road. As the silent Indian guru Meher Baba remarked on his chalkboard: "If drugs open the door, and leads disciples to me, that's fine. They should close it after that."

Really, one can use anything to meditate on—a mantra given to you by a teacher, your breath, OM/AUM . . . whatever. The mystical English writer Alan Watts asked the mythologist Joseph Campbell what kind of meditation he did, and Campbell responded, "I underline sentences." At that time, I was also reading *Be Here Now* by Ram Dass (aka Richard Alpert), who said that the most important thing about meditation is to *not* beat yourself up when you realize your busy mind has drifted away from the mantra (or your breath, or whatever you're using). Notice all those thoughts that race around in your cerebrum, and then just calmly return to your meditation.

The excitement was tangible one night at the Kinnara School: Ravi was in town and scheduled to give a talk to the students. With his girlfriend sitting behind him (as she did at all his concerts, playing the tamboura), the Maestro spoke of having the inner strength to sublimate the sexual drive into practicing one's instrument. This blew my twenty-year-old mind. Ravi practiced when he got horny! I'd heard of the yogis sending their sexual energy up their spines and around to the forehead for kundalini, but I knew this wasn't *my* path in life—especially in my youth when I was so aware of the all-encompassing throbbing in my pants. In America, we co-opt everything, so with the media mirroring my pressure below the belt, bad "sitar" music became the soundtrack for porn flicks. Ravi tried to stop it by suing the porn industry for the watered-down ragas, but the porn producers couldn't be cornered. Shankar's "sound of God" became the soundtrack of sex.

Our musical guru was also in town to play a concert at the prestigious Royce Hall on the UCLA college campus, where years before I'd seen John Coltrane. As students at the Kinnara School, we had the honor of sitting onstage with him as he left this world and entered the trance of Indian ragas. And Ravi did indeed leave this world. I sat close enough to notice toward the end of the two-hour musical journey that Ravi's fingertips were getting red from the constant picking. By the end, a little blood was dripping from several of his fingers, but the expression of joy on his face said that he neither noticed nor cared. There was that space again—a hedge against time.

Ravi went on to collaborate with the great classical violinist Sir Yehudi Menuhin. They met at a house concert, where Yehudi asked Ravi about yoga. The fiddler had a rigorous schedule and thought yoga might be a portable practice that could help him on the road. They eventually played together live, a successful duet in June 1966 at the Bath Musical Festival, which prompted a recording session. The result, *West Meets East*, won the 1967 Grammy Award for Best Chamber Music Performance—the first Grammy ever awarded to an Asian musician.

This historic pairing would help one half of the planet understand the other half. Yehudi turned the Western classical world on to the East, as Shankar was bringing the East to the West, even though classical Indian music, like Western jazz, was largely improvisational.

The East and the West have been colliding since the beginning of culture, trying to convince each other that their way is best. Ultimately, a synthesis seems the most ideal resolution of this debate. Each has something to teach the other. It's just that most of the time one or the other doesn't listen. An attempt was made by Swami Satchidananda, the Indian guru who spoke at the opening of Woodstock. He said that the West had been very helpful with teaching people how to make things and how to make them work. Now the East could teach others about spirituality.

Menuhin accurately described Ravi Shankar as

someone who is an immensely dedicated man of the greatest integrity. As a teacher, I know of no better. His total commitment to his art goes far beyond pure music making. For Ravi, all human activity, eating, dancing, doing exercise, is imbued with a symbolic value beyond reproach, and therefore it is all, in its own way, like some divine offering.

I think this sense of integrity rubbed off on me a little, because as Tavis Smiley said about my actions when I appeared on his PBS interview show, "To some it's courageous, to others it might be stupid, leaving a *whole* lot of money on the table." He was referring to my vetoing the use of our songs for commercials. I have tried to carry that torch forward into today's popular music, as I explained in an article I wrote for the *Daily Beast*:

At the risk of sounding grandiose, I will say that, to me, rock 'n' roll is sacred. It started out mid-twentieth century, and when dirt-poor Elvis bought his first Cadillac, that was his way of "blinging" the uptight '50s. Sixty years later, I said no to Cadillac, by vetoing the idea of a Doors song becoming the soundtrack to encourage folks to buy cruise mobiles. For all those years a tradition has been building. A tradition built on the idea that this music means something. And if compromised, its power could be lessened. We need to keep the flame burning, through hypocrisy, seeking truth.

Why did Jim Morrison say he'd smash a Buick on television if we did "Come on, Buick, Light My Fire?" Robby actually wrote that song, but Jim cared about our entire catalogue, the whole body of work we created. To quote Leonard Cohen, he was paying the rent in the "Tower of Song" for a long time. He knew what was sacred, and what was profane.

I'm not an atheist, I always say I believe in "the Mystery," because I hate fighting wars over the "G" word, but now I'm feeling that maybe music is my religion. It's been the single most important thru line in my 70+ years on this planet. So I don't want my mythology diluted. Look what that did to the

Native Americans. We took their spirit, and substituted the spirit with the bottle. I want my metaphysics potent. I want to get drunk and pass out on it (metaphorically). I want to crash against the rocks in ecstasy over the sound I hear. Praise be to Debussy's Sirens.

Quoting my second memoir (*The Doors: Unhinged*): "It's the Indian musical tradition of surrendering to a living guru who guides the student with discipline . . . but never abuse. And then it's the maturing of the relationship, where the student rises and sometimes surpasses the 'master,' who looks on with pride." Ravi's daughter Anoushka was a perfect example of this.

In his youth, for more than ten years, Shankar practiced his sitar six hours a day. Later in life, he admitted that his spine was twisted from sitting all that time. When spirit comes in, ecstasy overshadows everything. It seems that every profession comes with occupational hazards, whether it's wielding a jackhammer in the street or sitting on a drum stool. But for anyone doing something they can be proud of, the hazards are more likely to be tolerable. I support the idea of a skyscraper having a plaque that lists all the workers who erected it. They built the foundation, but the outside logo arrogantly brags only about the corporation that owns the building.

Later in life, Ravi said that playing music made the aches and pains disappear for those few hours of transcendental bliss. His huge, unbounded spirit carried him all the way through his ninety-six years of continual musical giving. Raviji was playing with extreme passion up until his final crossing. What a great mentor.

Chapter Twelve
Patti Smith
Vulnerability

Taking off your clothes is no cover-up . . .
it reveals great beauty.

She sat onstage at the Getty Museum next to her son. The two of them fumbled with their sheet music, dropping some of it on the floor. Their playlist got mixed up. Listeners might think this was unprofessional behavior, but something about their stage presence was utterly charming. Mother and son were doing a tribute to the late archivist, painter, and filmmaker Harry Smith. It didn't matter what song she sang. Something in that low, deep, never-ending vibrato went straight to the heart of the listener.

There was nothing like Patti Smith when she came on the scene at CBGB's in 1975. She dressed like a guy, which was unusual at the time, and she had utter disdain for anything phony.

The punks were blasting the hypocrisy creeping into the hippie ethos. In an interview with the *Guardian*, she reflected on this early incubation period.

> In 1974 a lot of our great voices had died. We'd lost Jimi Hendrix and Jim Morrison and Janis Joplin, and people like Robert Kennedy, Martin Luther King and Malcolm X. There were so many losses so quickly. These people who were building a political and cultural voice. And it seemed that rock 'n' roll was heading towards something different—something consumer-oriented and stadium-oriented. I felt new generations had to come and break everything apart. As Jim Morrison says, "Break on through to the other side." And I felt in the centre, not quite the old generation, not quite the new generation. I felt like the human bridge, and I just thought, you have to wake up. Wake them up.

In an interview just before he went to Paris to never return, Jim Morrison said: "Each generation wants new symbols, new people, new names. They want to divorce themselves from the preceding generation . . . they won't call it 'rock,' they'll invent some new name." Punk!

In 2013, I was writing along the same line of thought in my piece "Music Is My Religion" for the *Daily Beast*:

> This music has fed us spiritually, so when it seems to be losing its center, new movements come in to try to shore it up. Reinvigorate the muse. Each new creative wave that comes along seems to have to challenge the previous modus operandi. Elvis shocked Ike's generation with sexuality. The hippies were too

grubby for the early '60s crowd. The punks were too angry for the "flower power" folks. But all of these musical movements had the same message: vitality. Don't compromise the life force. Yes, to be human is to be humiliated, but in the face of that is spirit, which transcends the physical.

Before Patti had found her muse, she was hanging out with a young playwright named Sam Shepard. He would go on to win a Pulitzer Prize, while she became the Godmother of Punk. I'm a big fan of both artists. Being a drummer (with the Holy Modal Rounders), Shepard knew how to find the music in between the sentences. He also, in my opinion, captured the depth of human rage in most of his plays. Once when I was surfing the boob tube, I had to stop on John Malkovich doing Shepard's *True West*. I had *never* seen anything like that on TV or in the movies. As a young man, I could relate to the pent-up anger.

Patti started as a poet, with guitar backing. She gradually added all the elements to make a rock band, and then she charged ahead, spitting out words in staccato rhythm, honing her punk stance. Tall and gangly, with a lazy left eye, she redefined the role of what a rock star could be. Gaining her confidence from master painters like Picasso and Modigliani ("the women in their paintings look like me!"), Smith went beyond gender and raced up the charts with a couple of hit singles: "Because the Night" and "People Have the Power." She never sacrificed her integrity.

It was people like her who helped me when I was feeling very alone in my stance against my bandmates' desire to make money by licensing our songs for commercials. Smith admired Jim Morrison for his integrity, and her fierce purity as an artist gave me the courage to defend Jim's legacy. There's a through line here: fellow artists inspiring each other in their struggle to stay true to their original vision. For artists like Patti and Jim, money was secondary. The uncompromised work was the prize.

Then Patti did the unthinkable: she quit. Like Steve Martin, Björn Borg, and a very few others, she walked away from it all. Martin walked away from giant stadium shows and got into movies and playwriting. Patti moved to a suburb of Detroit, married Fred "Sonic" Smith of the MC5, and became a mother and housewife. What? The woman who penned "Jesus died for somebody's sins but not mine" had settled down in the Midwest?!

At first it seemed unthinkable, but it was a heroic move, resettling in the heartland. Maybe Patti was looking for the heart of America. She had not blasphemed with the Jesus quote. She just wanted to make her own mistakes, without expecting Christ to carry the burden that was hers.

Tragically, after almost a decade of living the "normal" family life, Fred died. Sometimes things are just not fair. But out of the ashes rose the CD *Gone Again*, which in my opinion is a masterpiece. Patti had also lost her brother Todd, and in these new songs she just flayed open her heart and let the grief pour out. They had some beautiful and uplifting moments too:

> But I look up
> and a rainbow appears
> like a smile from heaven
> and darling I can't
> help thinking that smile
> is yours

Fortunately for us, Patti Smith has a big heart. The first thing I said when we met backstage at the Getty was that *Gone Again* was a masterpiece. She introduced her son and said that the two of them loved The Doors. Mutual respect was all around. It was a thrill to meet her.

Since then, Patti Smith has written many books of poetry, had photo exhibits, painted, and more. She is a Renaissance woman. The prose in her memoir *Just Kids*, which won the National Book Award, is so personal and touching that you feel like you're living her life right next to her. Patti may be peaking later in life, but didn't the Chinese poets caution that you shouldn't publish too early? She is well seasoned, and I can't get enough of her creative fruits.

I've just returned from her "Horses" tour and am writing this at 1:00 a.m. after the concert, totally revitalized by her passion. At sixty-nine, Patti is channeling the essence of the muse and delivering it with as much power as any twenty-something rocker could hope to muster. She also understands dynamics, my personal favorite musical quality. She isn't afraid of silence. She isn't afraid of tenderness. She tells jokes onstage. She reads poetry. Patti doesn't put on a "show" per se. In her own words:

> When I'm writing, doing a drawing, writing a poem, I have an expectation of perfection, but when I am performing, singing for people, I don't care about any of that. For me the most important thing is communication. I'll communicate at the expense of . . . to get a laugh, I don't mind if I look foolish, I don't mind if I fail a little, make a mistake, as long as the people and I are in tune with each other.

In honor of her birthday, Patti covered the Jimi Hendrix tune "If 6 Was 9" at the "Horses" performance, and she screwed up the intro (which is very complex). She stopped the band and said that part of her charm is to make mistakes. She isn't worried about making mistakes in front of an audience. What I saw at that concert was a great artist showing everything she had—vulnerability and talent all in the same package.

A few years after her Getty Museum appearance, Patti had to recover from freezing in the middle of her performance of Bob Dylan's "Hard Rain's a-Gonna Fall" at the Nobel Prize awards ceremony in Stockholm, Sweden. Dylan had asked her to go receive the award and sing on his behalf at the ceremony. With the world watching, she messed up the second verse, but instead of trying to cover it up, she stopped. "One of the most difficult experiences of my performing life," Patti looked back. "I didn't forget the words, I've sung that song hundreds of times throughout my life—I froze."

She asked to begin again. "I just had to tell the truth. That's one thing I've learned as a performer. If you tell the truth, the audience is very forgiving. I just said I was very nervous, and could we start over. The next day, all of the Nobel laureates said they felt a kinship when I had such a rough moment." What would have been a disaster for anyone else, Patti turned into gold. She's an alchemist!

Lucy Weir, a fan, captures Patti Smith's essence perfectly in a YouTube post:

It was at the point at which she forgot the words, apologized with such beauty and humility, and began to sing again, that I really started to listen. Patti, you carry in your voice and in your heart the agonizing insight into the depth and terror of those who feel. Wonderful, sexy, original and mesmerising, but above all, breathtakingly brave. Break the rules! Make mistakes! Begin again! You are the heart of light. Thank you.

Patti is clearly a performer who works hard and who will keep offering us sustenance until she "breaks on through" and is welcomed over there. Angels have been hovering over her head ever since she entered this realm, and her connection with both worlds is apparent.

An old proverb says that spirit won't come down unless there is a song. I think the transcendental Persian poet Hafiz was talking not only about all of us but especially about Patti when he wrote: "Wayfarer, I can see that the pattern upon your soul has the signature of the divine upon it. Wayfarer, if you had the eyes of a seer, you could see how Hafiz is always kneeling by your side, humming playful tunes."

So, reader, find the time to paint, or sing, or play an instrument. When you do, someone else will be in the room with you.

I will close by singing to Patti the letters sung by Aretha— much R-E-S-P-E-C-T.

Chapter Thirteen

Robert Nesta Marley

Rasta Man Vibration

Jah is within.

My grandson Rio's middle name is the same as Robert Nesta Marley's. Rio Nesta lives in the Northwest, an area not heavily populated by African Americans, but an area, at least in the cities, of progressive politics and a love of reggae.

I was very fortunate to be recording in Jamaica before reggae hit the States. It all began back in the spring of '69 when The Doors started and finished a tour in Miami. All of the next twenty cities on our schedule had canceled after Jim Morrison allegedly exposed himself. So three of the four Doors went to nearby Jamaica for a week's vacation.

I had no idea that trip was going to be the beginning of a permanent attraction to the music and culture of a tough, independent Caribbean island—an island you can drive around in four hours, but also an island that for fifty years has produced music whose impact on the entire world has been massive, both directly and indirectly.

While I was walking along a road on the north shore of Jamaica with Robby, the police pulled up and stopped us. They asked what we were doing, where we were from, and why we looked the way we did. (It was the length of our hair that got their attention.) We said we were on vacation, we were from Los Angeles, and everyone back home looked like us. (Well, everyone in Hollywood anyway.) They reluctantly let us go, and we continued on our way to score some ganja. Obviously, dreadlocks hadn't surfaced on the island yet, but herb had been there for years.

Jim was supposed to bring along his girlfriend Pam, but they had a fight in LA, so she never made it to Miami. They were going to stay at this old plantation house at the top of a tropical hill, but Jim ended up staying there a few days alone before he joined Robby and me at our place. He said that his short stay at the plantation house had been "spooky." He described sitting in the dining room at the end of a long table, eating, while the help sat in chairs along the walls, waiting to be called upon. The bedrooms had lace curtains over the beds to keep the bugs out. It was all pretty intense for a boy from Florida.

Robby and I and our girlfriends had a house with a cook and a caretaker. At night we'd have chicken, peas, and rice—a

Jamaica specialty—and then Tom, the caretaker, would bring out his 45s and his spliffs (marijuana joints). That's when we were exposed to early ska music, a predecessor of reggae. "Tonight" by John Holt was a favorite of everyone; we would play it ten or fifteen times in a row. The rhythm track had an infectious groove. The cook would dance, looking sooo cool. Her movements were very subtle, and I couldn't believe the rhythm in her body. Tom would crack a big smile, showing his lack of front teeth, and just snap his fingers. He was in the "pocket."

At the time we were maybe too young to fully grasp the fraught racial politics on the island. We didn't get to Mo Bay (Montego Bay), let alone Kingston, on this trip, but something must have been brewing there. With about one million blacks out of work and only a handful of British whites still controlling the economy, the poverty level was very high. Jamaica had received its independence from England only eight years before, and you could tell that the locals preferred the Americans to the British. But a resentment of all tourists was soon to come.

While we were on the island, our manager called from LA and said that warrants had arrived for Jim's arrest. He'd been charged, incredibly, with lewd and lascivious behavior: simulating oral copulation and indecent exposure at the Miami concert.

I couldn't believe the charges. Yes, Jim had been drunk, but simulating oral copulation? The charge must have been alluding to when Jim got down on his knees to get a closer look at Robby's fingers as he played guitar. Robby didn't play with a pick; instead, he plucked with his long fingernails (which he grew to play flamenco). His hand looked like a crab crawling across the strings. Jim didn't play an instrument, so he was en-amored with musicians. I too was enamored with Robby's gui-tar technique.

And if Jim had whipped it out, why didn't they arrest him on the spot? Why were the police so friendly after the concert? Jim had grabbed one of the security cops' hats during the per-formance and put it on his head. They came backstage, and we paid them for the loss of property. Later we found out that politicians were obviously trying to nail Jim as an example of moral decay. Or maybe it was some right-wing bullshit plot. Fucking politics.

Four years down the road, I found myself on the way to Jamaica again to record a new group Robby and I had organized—The Butts Band. Morrison had died two years earlier. The three remaining Doors had recorded a couple of albums after Jim's death, but it was over. Our spark was gone. Ray was trying to start a solo career, and Robby and I were feeling frustrated at not being able to play, so we started a new group.

We were recording in London when our bassist, Phil Chen, suggested that we finish the album in Jamaica, where he could visit his parents. Phil was of Chinese descent, but born in Ja-maica, and his accent was so thick I couldn't understand him, even though he was speaking English. Reggae was bubbling up from under the bricks of Brixton, a poor suburb of London, and Phil turned us on to the new sounds.

We were in Jamaica one month. That visit left an impres-sion on me that endures to this day. We got off the plane and were met by a VW bus, courtesy of Dynamic Sound Studios in Kingston. On the seat was a shopping bag full of ganja and a quart bottle of some dark brown liquid called "roots." It was a mixture of white rum, herbs, and God knows what else. We all took swigs and grimaced because it tasted like liquid fertilizer. The Jamaicans laughed, saying that many locals ended up in hospitals from drinking too much of the stuff.

Chris Blackwell, president of Island Records, had loaned us Strawberry Hill, his house high up in the Blue Mountains overlooking Kingston. The view from there was astounding. We smoked a lot of grass and stared down at the "concrete jungle" below. Our bodyguard, Maxie, assigned by the studio, always used to say, "He's away," when I looked stoned. The studio felt that we needed a local companion in case there was any trouble. You could feel the potential for trouble as we drove down to Kingston every day, passing shantytowns full of poor people.

Another change since I'd been there several years before was shocking. The more radical locals had let their kinky black hair grow, having sworn never to touch it with a comb again. Dreadlocks. Natty dreadlocks. It was a one-way trip. The only way out, once you let it go, was a pair of scissors. You had to be brave to do it. They had also taken up the Rastafarian religion, whose adherents believed that Africa was the "promised land" and marijuana a sacrament.

The Rastas were pretty frightening-looking at first, but they were friendly to us visiting honkies. The police came down heavy on them, though. The main source of income for the Rastas was selling grass, so they were a target. It reminded me of the tension between the hippies and the police in the late sixties in the States.

One day there was a big fight over studio time between a new reggae singer, Jimmy Cliff, and us. He wanted the studio earlier in the afternoon, and we had it booked. He was so hostile that we didn't put up much of a fight. I had mixed feelings over this dispute: I knew we were in the right, but Cliff at that moment was expressing many years of oppression and frustration. He was directing his anger toward these white musicians who were coming to Jamaica to record. Cliff's musicians came in, and we watched them record the track for a song called "Fundamental Reggae." When they hit that groove, my uneasiness disappeared immediately and I felt lucky to be there.

We had a big party at Strawberry Hill, and Maxie brought his coveted collection of 45s. We heard practically the entire history of Jamaican music. Bob Marley's "Wailers" affected me the most. Bob expressed the whole gamut of human emotions, from the tenderness of "No Woman No Cry" to the greed of organized religion in "Get Up, Stand Up." Marley fearlessly confronted old school monotheism head-on. He sang "Get up, stand up, stand up for your right" with such conviction that the collection cups that filled the coffers of churches were quivering. The Butts Band did a cover version of this song, fusing rock and reggae.

When I got back to LA, Kenny Edwards, Linda Ronstadt's bass player, and his wonderful songwriter girlfriend Karla Bonoff came over one night, and we played reggae records and talked for hours. I was so caught up in the "roots, Rasta, reggae" adventure I'd been on that I think they caught my enthusiasm. (Later Linda had a giant hit with "Many Rivers to Cross" by Jimmy Cliff . . . so they got the vibe!)

"No, it's not called 'Reggie,'" I explained. "It's REG-GAY." I told them how reggae bass players play in a loose solo style, leaving lots of spaces. Rumor had it that Jamaican musicians turned the beat around because they had such poor reception from American radio stations that eventually they thought it was played that way, but I don't buy that. Marley wrote the lyric "playing a rhythm fighting against da system." The man knew what he was doing.

The son of Captain Norval Marley, who married a young Jamaican girl named Cedalla Booker, Robert Nesta Marley was born in his grandfather's house. He knew that "no woman, no cry" was "improper" English for "baby, don't cry," but that was his point: to upset the status quo, to sing the way people actually spoke on the street, to find a new way. Marley's caring heart was open for all to see. The Wailers named themselves after all the residents in Trenchtown crying (wailing) about their circumstances.

In fact, Bob invented a new language. The "crazy bald-heads" (businessmen) were ruining the planet, turning it into "Babylon." He purposely used slang and "bad" syntax, to major effect. Like rappers, when you're saying powerful stuff, the power is multiplied if you can camouflage it, forcing the uninformed listener to figure out the message through new language. That subversive approach can also help a radical message reach the mainstream. "Something's happening here / But you don't know what it is / Do you, Mr. Jones?" Bob Dylan wrote in the midsixties.

What blew the minds of us drummers was the way reggae turned the beat around. My scientist mentor, Neil deGrasse Tyson, says that math is the language of the universe. It's the language of music too. Musical notation is just a bunch of math. What turns it into music is the feeling you put in between the numbers. Usually the bass drum is played on the first and third beats in a 4/4 rock 'n' roll groove. In reggae, it plays on the second and fourth beats. So when you do a fill, to accent the end of a section, you usually slam in with the bass drum on one afterwards, to signal the start of a new bar. In reggae, on the other hand, you wait another beat and come in on two. That was big. The Wailers' skin beater, Carlton Barrett, was a master of this style, which became known as "one-drop" rhythm. He would also turn off his snares (the wires under the snare drum), tighten the head, and whack the drum like a timbale (Latin drum), making a *very* unique sound.

The signature guitar rhythm (*cica-cica*) in reggae comes from using too much echo, which they stumbled onto in the studio by mistake. I guess there are no mistakes. Either that or leave room for them and the mistakes will teach you. As Miles said, "If you play a bad note, the next note you play will determine whether the first one was bad or good."

Six months later, back home in LA, I was looking in the calendar section of the *LA Times* and saw that "The Wailing Wailers" were playing second bill to Cheech and Chong at the Roxy. Could it be the same Wailers I was exposed to on a record in Jamaica? The Wailers with Bob Marley, Peter Tosh, and the Barrett Brothers, the tightest rhythm section in reggae? As it turned out, it *was* them. I knew this was going to be special.

Bob and crew were second bill because reggae still hadn't hit the States. Chris Blackwell was there, and Kenny Edwards, but no one else I knew. It was a full house, but they hadn't come for the reggae band. What was reggae anyway? I didn't think there were enough West Indians in southern California to support reggae like there were in London or on the East Coast.

The music started with the primal upside-down beat as the curtain slowly rose. Marley was down on his knees on the side of the stage playing a huge bass drum. (His performance was rather subdued compared to when I saw him a year later, but I was still spellbound.) I saw a black guy in the balcony looking kind of confused, trying to figure out where the beat was. This wasn't funk or soul music. This was culture shock. I'm sure the Wailers' dreadlocks shocked the brother in the balcony as well. Sporting a large Afro, he was there to enjoy the pot-laced humor of the Spanish-Chinese duo from Canada, and he couldn't dance to this weird backward reggae groove.

It's confusing to all of us when an artist is doing something so ahead of its time. Dylan has "confused" us many, many times with his brilliant artistic leaps, without a net and always ahead of the curve.

Afterwards, I went backstage because I had heard from Blackwell that Marley liked the Butts Band version of "Get Up, Stand Up." The door was open, but the amount of ganja wafting from the room was so thick that it felt like I had to break through a barrier to enter. The vibe from the band was kinda like *What the fuck is this white guy doing in here?* Marley knew I was a member of the rock band that covered his song, and he gave me a friendly nod. This was a year before Eric Clapton covered "I Shot the Sheriff." I made a quick exit.

The next two times I saw them at the Roxy, they were the headliners. On the first occasion, they were amazing. Like our Jamaican cook on the island, Marley seemed to be inside the music when he moved (not dissimilar to how the brilliant Gustavo Dudamel conducts the LA Philharmonic, his whole body seeming to inhabit the sounds). The house was sold out, and Marley had the crowd dancing on the tabletops. The second time I saw them, they were a little off. My idol was human after all. After this engagement, they were about to make the jump from playing clubs to performing in concerts before larger audiences, and I knew they would be successful.

The larger new audiences in the United States were mostly white kids, and The Wailers won their affection easily. I knew that, like Jimi Hendrix, Marley wanted to reach the American black audiences, but it didn't happen on a large scale while he was still alive. I think the artistry of both Hendrix and Marley was too universal to be kept in one category. For instance, the Police would chase down an incredible reggae-influenced rock groove, with major help from their drummer Stewart Copeland. Over time Marley's lyrics have been totally embraced by people of color, who came to realize that he was an early warrior, spearheading the fight against oppression.

I have always liked a little politics with my art, so when there was an assassination attempt on Marley before a concert and he still managed to get onstage and perform, my admiration for him doubled. Later he bravely wrote "Ambush in the Night," a song about "all guns aiming at me." Several years later, I heard that Marley had been hospitalized for cancer. I wondered if it had anything to do with chain-smoking his sacrament. I didn't pay the news much mind and thought it might have been only a rumor. I couldn't imagine Bob Marley ill. He seemed untouchable.

I was sitting in a coffee shop eating breakfast when I saw the headlines at the newsstand, "Bob Marley Dies." I was shell-shocked. I'd had no idea his illness was that serious. It turned out that he had skin cancer on his toe that had been left un-treated for too long and eventually spread. He was only thirty-six, my age at the time.

No one around me seemed to have an inkling that a major force in music, as well as a great humanitarian, had died. I got in the car and put on a Wailers tape. It started in the middle of a verse of a song called "Burnin' and Lootin'": "How many riv-ers do we have to cross, / Before we can talk to the boss?"

I thought to myself, *Marley is finally going to meet Jah* (the Rastafarian God). The next song to come on was "Rasta Man Chant," the first song I ever saw them perform, at the Roxy Club in Los Angeles. The last verse goes: "One bright morning when my work is over, man will fly away home." Bob Marley is home, but his spirit will remain for a long time down here in Babylon.

Chapter Fourteen
Airto Moreira
Percussion Healer

Your hands know more than your brain.

orn into a family of folk healers in Brazil, Airto Moreira's musical talent was obvious very early on. At age six, he was asked to do his own radio show. At thirteen, he was asked to play drums in a band when the drummer wasn't available. He said he'd try, having played hand percussion already for many years. He rocked, and soon he was playing on the streets for change.

Eventually migrating to New York City, Airto hooked up with the greatest jazz trumpeter of all time: Miles Davis. Together with other future jazz greats, such as Keith Jarrett and Chick Corea, they created the genre called "jazz-fusion."

Moreira participated in creating the seminal jazz recording *Bitches Brew* in 1970. Back in the day, I was blessed to see that ensemble live, and what a brew they stirred up. Miles was his usual elusive self, while the band burned a hole through the stage. Backstage after the show, an overenthusiastic critic was waxing rhapsodic about his brilliant performance, when Miles snapped, "I don't care how I played . . . how did I look?" That reminded me of the kind of responses Bob Dylan threw at journalists.

After leaving Miles, the mad stick beater joined Weather Report, recording several important albums and touring the world with them. Bruce Botnick, the Doors' longtime recording engineer, told an insightful story about working on one of those albums. They had finished a take, and Bruce asked the never-humble Joe Zawinul if they wanted to do another. "Are you kidding! Bruce, this is Weather Report. We only do one take." Arrogant, yes, but they were the best.

Airto eventually moved on to Chick Corea's group Return to Forever, another vital jazz force in the world of fusion. Then, in 1974, Airto formed his own group, along with his mate, Flora Purim, and they recorded many albums for big record companies.

I went down to see them live at the Whisky, where we had been the house band many years before. When Airto performs, he is surrounded by percussion instruments that look like artifacts from a rainforest, and he can sound like one too. He has percussion instruments from around the world. There are no borders around the well of his creativity. Picking up just one instrument, the *pandeiro* (tambourine), Airto performed a ten-minute symphony of such musical brilliance that I felt, along with the audience, as if we had just experienced every human emotion possible.

The world-renowned architect Frank Gehry says that musicians and architects are similar. "Architecture is about making feelings with inert materials, and music is making masterpieces with spatial sound environments."

Through miraculous handwork accompanied by his chanting, shouts of encouragement to himself, and primal shamanic grunts, Airto created a kind of séance. He is a hypnotist. Gehry again: "In designing a building, you're trying to create a feeling, and musicians and composers also talk about trying to create a feeling." Airto started slow, weaving a sound web, and then you were caught; there was no escaping this web. Next he drove you through all the sensations of an entire carnival in Brazil, before guiding you back down and letting you go.

With an ear tuned to playing exactly the right sound at the right moment, Airto has been the first choice for many record producers, bandleaders, and songwriters. Quincy Jones, Herbie Hancock, Paul Simon, Carlos Santana, Gil Evans, Chicago, and the Grateful Dead all know that what Moreira hears in their compositions is the right thing to add. Film composers have also jumped on the Airto bandwagon and captured his sounds for *The Exorcist*, *Last Tango in Paris*, and *Apocalypse Now*. Francis Ford Coppola made very effective use of the Doors' music, combined with the contribution of the master percussionist, in *Apocalypse Now*.

Airto's work on films represents only a small number of the musical contributions he has made over the last four decades. In fact, Airto's impact is so strong that *Downbeat* magazine added a percussion category to its polls of readers and critics. He has won those polls twenty times since 1973. In a nutshell, Airto is the world's greatest living percussionist. In 2002, the president of Brazil awarded Airto and Flora the Order of Rio Blanco, one of the country's highest honors.

Okay, so that was one of the most impressive bios ever, right? But what is really impressive is the soul of the man. Granted, he comes from a country with an impressive soul: there seem to be many people in Brazil who walk down the street singing a song, enjoying life. But *everyone* who has worked with this guy loves him, because he emanates love.

I once saw him perform with a mentally challenged youth at a fundraiser, and it was magic. As usual, being the openhearted guy he is, Airto instantly created community with the kid. The two of them reveled in the world of sound, healing each other's pain by having a musical conversation. Moreira would do a phrase, and his new partner would answer. It was clear that the audience was thrilled to be in on the conversation, because everyone was listening so intently. The master's caring compassion and patience toward the youth were completely charming, and the two of them produced some great music.

What Airto has taught me is that staying extremely focused and playing the perfect beat in the right place is as powerful as showing off the flashiest techno flurry. One note can be as musical as one hundred if it's played where it should be.

I saw Airto perform recently, just after he had undergone not one but two hip replacement operations. He couldn't walk up stairs, and he slumped over his drum stool, but like Ravi Shankar, when he played, he transcended his pain.

We talked about *Apocalypse Now* as he reached out his hand to shake mine after the last set. And shake he did, his hand

My mom painting her last painting.
She passed four days later at the age
of ninety-four.
Ann Densmore

A hug from my rhythm bro, Elvin Jones, at Slugs.
Lin Curiel

© *Fantality Corp.*

"The blue bus is calling us."
Paul Ferrara

Van Morrison.
© 2020 Richard E. Aaron

Emil Richards. He played with Sinatra, Ravi
Shankar, George Harrison…and me!
Celeste Radocchia

Ravi Shankar: The Godfather of World Music.
Alan Kozlowski

Two rockers (Lou Reed and yours truly) talk politics at BookExpo in New York, circa 1991.
Images Press/Getty Images

The Doors' rhythm section, driving the Blue Bus.
Henry Diltz

Jammin' with my poetic father figure, Robert Bly.
John Densmore Collection

© 2020 Richard E. Aaron

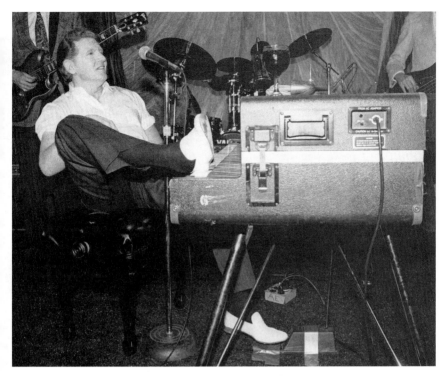

"For those who like me, God love ya. For rest—have a heart attack."
© 2020 Richard E. Aaron

The Rocker and The Dude (as in Gustavo Dudamel).
Music for longhairs.
Alan Ronay

Ram Dass and me, opening the
Doors of Perception.
John Densmore Collection

One of the calmest sets of eyes on the planet.
Rob Kim/Getty Images

quivering with a pronounced tremor. Then he picked up a percussion instrument a friend of mine had given him that night. All of a sudden his fingers quickened, coming to life as virtuosity entered his hands. Hands that had spent a lifetime honing his craft. Hands that had an intelligence beyond the rest of his body—beyond the rest of us—took over and tapped into some kind of universal energy. Airto's hands channeled the cosmos to give us all a gift. The gift of sound.

Maybe he was able to tap into the source of sound. The first sound. I don't want to get biblical, but in the beginning there was nothing, and then there was sound. Whether it was the Big Bang or the Creator snapping his or her fingers, the whole thing started with a sound. Airto is a composite of all the percussionists throughout all time. Some of his instruments are very old, and the vibrations emitted from them give a sense of history. You can feel the depth of the ages in them. His playing on them taps something ancient, deep, and primal down in your psyche.

What a blessing that, at the time of this writing, this man is still among us, walking, breathing, sharing his magic. It has been such an honor to spend a little time with him. If you think I'm over the top here, go to YouTube and listen to Moreira at the 2003 Modern Drummer Festival. Then you'll understand.

Chapter Fifteen

Jerry Lee Lewis

Killer Energy

Passion is the key to creativity.

When I was a kid, I couldn't get enough of Jerry Lee Lewis's boogie-woogie piano. I listened to "Great Balls of Fire" over and over, although I didn't know what the lyrics meant. I mean, I knew it was sexual, but couldn't figure out the literal meaning. I knew "Whole Lotta Shakin' Goin' On" was about doin' the nasty. But did "Great Balls of Fire" mean his girl lit a match under his testicles?

The thing that got me, even as a thirteen-year-old, was the *energy* coming off of Jerry Lee's records. They made me feel like I just drank a couple of cups of strong coffee, and I was still too young to even have a taste for java. There was no way you could listen to the man from Ferriday, Louisiana, and not move. Your body would not allow you to remain sitting in your chair.

I finally saw a clip of JLL live and was blown away. Lewis would occasionally pound the keys with the heel of his foot or kick the piano bench aside and play standing, raking his hands up and down the keyboard. It sounded like he was breaking his fingers going up and down those eighty-eight keys. He must have had calluses on *all* of his fingers because the way he slid from the bass notes to the high notes and back made it seem as if his extremities were made of wood instead of flesh. When he would turn around and sit his butt on the keyboard and jab rhythm, he was playing in time, like a percussion instrument.

These antics really turned on a young teenager like me, but later as a musician I realized that Lewis wasn't sacrificing any musicality doing these crowd-pleasing pranks. Like his contemporaries Little Richard and Chuck Berry, Jerry Lee is a showman, an entertainer. Not that he's a con man. The substance of what he's doing is great, but he's really good at selling what he does.

Recently some people have been calling *me* an icon (probably because I'm getting so old!), but, yes, I can still con too. After all, what is art but a con? You can't repair a car with a song. You can't fix plumbing with a painting. So art is like a sleight of hand, a kind of magic; a séance that, when done well, can imbue people with soul. It's hard to pin down why, but art seems to inspire people, some to the point of being willing to die for it. In fact, some governments, if they sense a subversive threat to their regime's philosophy, are willing to kill songwriters to stop the inspiration they spread.

Jerry Lee had several big hits, but unfortunately the passion he expressed in his music showed up in his personal life when he married his thirteen-year-old cousin. Not a good PR move. His career took a major nosedive until many years later, when he broke into country music. That was when we met him.

The Doors had become big enough to be able to dictate who we wanted as our opening act. Just as the Rolling Stones had given a nod to the blues great B. B. King by having him start their show, we wanted to acknowledge the '50s rock 'n' rollers who had fed us and furthered the genre.

Several months before, our attempt to honor an earlier musician we admired during our Hollywood Bowl gig had backfired. Since we loved the song "I Walk the Line," we suggested Johnny Cash, who was relatively unknown at the time to the younger generation, as our opener. Musicians certainly knew how talented he was, but this was before his TV show aired, and the masses hadn't caught up yet. Obviously, the promoters hadn't either, because their response was: "We're not hiring an ex-con . . . he's a felon."

Playing the eighteen-thousand-seat Inglewood Forum, we tried again. "Touch Me" had quickly reached number one, so our clout was stronger and the promoter agreed to let us have Jerry Lee Lewis start the show. He said nobody would know who Jerry Lee was, but we ignored that comment. My book *Riders on the Storm* sets the stage: "We were thrilled that Mr. Lewis was 'acceptable.' They said he wouldn't draw, but we didn't care. They said he only played country music now, but we didn't care." Actually, we did have our managers suggest to his manager that he throw in some of the old rock hits, which we felt would elicit a more favorable response from our audience.

At the sound check, we finally came face to face with "The Killer." He was known for combing his hair in the middle of his show, combing it in between piano notes, and lo and behold, he whipped the black instrument out of his back pocket and gave his blond hair a couple of swipes before shaking my hand. What a showman! *Riders* again:

"Can my boys borrow your drums?" "Sure, Jerry Lee," I smiled. He turned to Robby. "Can we borrow a gittar?" "What kind of guitar do you want? I have several," Robby replied. "Any old rock 'a day Fender gittar," Jerry Lee quipped. Apparently Mr. Lewis's band showed up at the gig without any instruments.

Jerry Lee did more than oblige the audience with some of the old rock hits—he played a whole set of them. Unfortunately, some of the groupies were shouting, "Jim, Jim, Doors, Doors," during The Killer's show. Too often fans and audiences don't understand that musicians honor those who came before them. We came to love the art forms of the previous generation and learned our craft by studying and admiring their work.

Artists aren't the only ones who do this. Those of us who were young during the '60s were completely lied to by our parents about the Vietnam conflict, so those of our generation who became parents listened more to their kids. And if our kids listened to us, they weren't programmed to support another war.

Jerry Lee didn't seem to mind the catcalls, though. In fact, he seemed to thrive on the confrontation with the hecklers. At the end of his set, The Killer jumped on top of the grand piano and made a farewell speech: "FOR THOSE OF YOU WHO

LIKED ME, GOD LOVE YA. FOR THE REST OF YOU, I HOPE YOU HAVE A HEART ATTACK!" We apologized for the heckling as he came offstage as we complimented him. I mimicked Ed Sullivan's idiosyncratic pronunciation, saying, "Great *shoe*, really great *shoe*."

Jerry Lee seemed to have enjoyed himself, and to not be bothered by the friction with the audience. If you're going to take on Jerry Lee Lewis, you better be ready, 'cause he'll come back at you with more than you dished out. I was very pleased that we jump-started the look back to the roots of rock 'n' roll, and it was an honor to hang a little with the man who hung with Elvis and Chuck Berry.

As a kid, I was seduced by Jerry Lee's dynamics. He would get real soft on "wiggle around just a little bit" in "Whole Lotta Shakin'," pulling the listener in. Then, in the last chorus, he would blast you. I was taking this all in, not knowing that later I would get real soft in the song "The End," then blast the last section. The dynamics in classical music had the same effect on me. It was so emotional to have loud *and* soft, as well as everything in between.

Jerry Lee's music runs the gamut of human feelings. If you put on a JLL record (or stream his music, or use whatever delivery system floats your boat), you will pick up so much sheer energy listening to him that you'll immediately find the time to go directly into your creative space and work out! Jerry Lee Lewis was another one of my teachers in the "school of rock," and he can be yours too. The Killer "killed" me, and he will "kill" you too—if you let him.

Chapter Sixteen

Joseph Campbell

The Hero's Journey

Joyful participation in the sorrows of the world

O kay, Joseph Campbell isn't a musician per se, but if, as I've said before, a sentence reads like a musical question, Campbell's writing is a symphony.

I didn't know him well enough to call him "Joe," unlike my friend Phil Cousineau, who edited the companion book to *The Hero's Journey*, a documentary film on Campbell's life. My first encounter with the man who inspired George Lucas to write *Star Wars* was at the Jung Institute in West Los Angeles, where Campbell was giving a lecture with slides. Although I'd read

Hero with a Thousand Faces, I was new to the world of mythology. What I didn't know was that I was meeting a teacher who would feed my spirituality big-time.

What I took away from Campbell's talk was that many similarities exist between the world's religions. This was in the old days before there was the internet to connect the global village. So how did these connections come about? Well, Mr. Campbell hinted, perhaps all the world's mythologies have so much in common because they are true. Maybe mythologies point to threads that link us all. After all, such connections exist in the biological world. At a Bioneers Conference, I heard the mycologist Paul Stamets speak about the underground network of bacteria worldwide. We're walking on a fungi internet! As the slogan for that conference put it: "It's all alive, it's all connected, it's all intelligent, it's all relatives."

When I was a kid, I asked my parents, if there is only one God, why are there so many religions? My mom, who went to mass every Sunday, said that there were many wonderful religions, but that not all of them got you into heaven. I was young then, and she later rescinded that idea. Still, that kind of early experience may partly explain why a lot of my friends are Jewish: I was developing a preference for outsiders, and Jews were "the chosen few." There's wisdom on the edge.

"Joe" could name all the world's faiths and tell you how the religious deities arose. Even with his sense of the parallels between religions, Mr. Campbell, like my mom, was a devout Catholic. Another expert in comparative religions, Huston Smith, also thought that you needed an old school tradition to anchor your psyche. Even though the esteemed Mr. Smith imbibed lysergic acid with the likes of Ram Dass and Aldous Huxley, he still clung to his Christian faith.

I have found that after my own direct experience with the quantum world through psychedelics, organized religions seem dated. Still, I'm actually a little jealous of the security that my mom and Joseph Campbell and Huston Smith got from being wrapped in the arms of Jesus. I just can't accept it myself. As a musician, I know Jesus is definitely the lead singer, but clearly Buddha is on drums. And Allah is probably the lead guitarist, milking those strings for all he's got.

I'm not making light of these visionaries here; I really do borrow from all the world's great religions, and get fed various ingredients. It's similar to my love of world music, which feeds me sounds from all the various cultures. Even if I don't understand the language being sung, I still get the essence of the culture. In religion, Hinduism's multi-limbed gods of jealousy, wrath, sex, and so on, have helped me feel like I'm not crazy for having those feelings myself. I find the likenesses between belief systems reassuring, but in the end I prefer a patchwork cosmology.

I had heard that Campbell was taken to a Grateful Dead concert and saw some magic there, even though he had said that rock music never appealed to him. "They hit a level of humanity," he noted, "that makes everybody at one with each other." I don't know if Mr. Campbell knew the quantity of drugs being taken at these concerts, but I agree that "this awakening the common humanity is a quite different rhythm system from that of marching to the bugle of 'Onward Christian Soldiers'!"

Concurring with the highly imaginative novelist Tom Robbins, who said that Campbell's writings "often turned the spit in my cognitive barbecue," I went to a Joseph Campbell conference at the Esalen Institute in Big Sur, California, to hang for a while with the scholar. Sitting in the dining room, surrounded by groupies of all ages (some attractive young women, some older sage types), "Joe" charmed everybody with many stories from his reading and travels.

The venerated mythologist said that the monotheistic myth is crumbling and that it might take a few hundred years for a new myth to fully form. On the same subject, the Dalai Lama ruminated, "I believe deeply that we must find, all of us together, a new spirituality. This new concept ought to be elaborated alongside the religions in such a way that all people of goodwill could adhere to it." Campbell thinks that ultimately this new myth will replace the old one.

It is interesting that when Joseph Campbell wrote about the mythology of the "hero's journey," it was ending. The independent loner, fighting by himself, is facing the setting sun. The new religion, perhaps, is framed by a *group*. Whether it tells the story of combating climate change or fighting criminal injustice, the new mythology is more likely to raise up a group than a single savior.

As I listened to Campbell's talk, I realized that what I've been doing is combining a little mythology from the Hindu world, with its many diverse gods, with Native American reverence for the earth and sky as mother and father gods. At that point, I got paranoid and thought the new age vibe at Esalen was getting to me. But my paranoia subsided when I reminded myself that here was an extremely educated man who was devoted to his wife Jean Erdman and who wouldn't even go down to the Esalen mineral baths because they were clothing-optional.

The poet Robert Bly invited Campbell to attend one of his men's groups and continue with his wonderful stories, which illustrated how to live here on Mother Earth. The meetings were usually held at campgrounds. Bly told me that Joe said he'd come, but only if he had a nice room; he wasn't going to "rough it." He also wasn't a vegetarian, citing a Native American story about the covenant between the buffalo and a tribe: the tribe members would profusely thank the animal before taking its life for sustenance. Most importantly, they never took too much, only enough for the coming winter.

When the film documentary on Campbell's life, *The Hero's Journey*, was premiered at the Directors Guild in Hollywood, I was invited to be on a panel after the screening. My anticipation doubled when I realized that the chair with my name on it was right next to the chair for "The Man." I knew the maverick scholar was in his eighties, but didn't know that this would be his next-to-last public appearance.

It was a very warm discussion, mainly full of accolades about the mythologist. I commented that "I didn't know I was performing at a Dionysian festival rite when playing drums with The Doors until I read this guy."

"This religious system has to do with the awakening of your nature, and that's the one that your art," he retorted, pointing at me, "is operating on."

That felt good to hear. Later he complimented my clan again: "I think that the Grateful Dead are the best answer today to the atom bomb."

At the end there was a Q&A with the audience. I nervously raised my hand when the moderator, Richard Beban, said we had time for one more question. I knew Campbell had hung out a little with my fellow musicians, but his presence still intimidated me. Or maybe I was a little scared about challenging him with my question.

Densmore: I'm going to try and put you on the spot. (*JC rolled his eyes.*)

Campbell: I knew that moment would come. (*Then he smiled. That was a relief.*)

Densmore: The essence of the world is sorrow, and the trick is "joyful participation in the sorrows of the world. Say yes to it and watch it blow up. The world is okay, all rests in God." Right?

Campbell: That's a very nice lecture. I go with it all the way. (*I plucked this excerpt from one of JC's books.*)

Densmore: Right. So for me, that gives me peace. But I feel like if I completely embrace that statement— well, I feel like I shouldn't completely embrace that statement until the moment before I die. Otherwise, I think there's a danger of complacency. You know, I want to go out and fight against Fascists like Hitler or the nuclear thing. And I wonder whether this undermines me.

Campbell: This is the problem with the self and the ego. At the deep base, at the eternal center, this is the way it is. And how can my moral ideas be brought in accord with it? At the same time we see we have all the money over there, and we have poor people here. I can work for the human values as being not the essential ones but the potential ones.

At heart, I would say, no matter what happens, everything is okay. Suppose the world blows up—so what. You know, just absolutely, so what. But in terms of human values that's a real calamity! (*much laughter*) So in my human nature I'm going to do what I can to keep it from blowing up. My books have been working in that direction.

All life is sorrowful. You are not going to change that. The thing is, you must participate. That is the act of the Buddhist saying: "Life is joyful participation in the sorrows of the world." Do you see what I mean? You get a point of view, you get a—what can we call it—a non-egoistic, nonjudgmental point of view. And so go into the play and play a part. And at the same time know that this is a shadow reflex.

I was reading in one of the Sanskrit texts recently, because in your old age, my dear friends, in your free time, you go back to what fed you most in your youth and childhood. So I found myself working again on the *Bhagavad Gita* and the Puranas and brushing up on my Sanskrit. And there was something that came out of this that I had read before and it had never struck me this way.

The eternal cannot change. It's not touched by time. And as soon as you have a historical act, a movement, you're in time. The world of time is a reflex of the energy of what is eternal. But the eternal is not touched by what is here. So the whole doctrine of sin is a false doctrine. It has to do with time. Your eternal character is not touched.

You are redeemed.

WOW. That's all my mind could think. The Man left to a standing ovation, and he "broke on through" to the eternal a couple of weeks later.

When I recently reread Campbell's answer to this last question of mine, I also had a revelation that hadn't struck me the first time I heard it. My life has been full of sound, and as I've gotten older, the sound of silence has become more appealing. Silence is much louder than I thought. When Leonard Cohen spent five years at the Mount Baldy Zen monastery, his name was "Jikan." It means the silence between two thoughts. The lost home that I'm looking for, that all of us are looking for, is inside. Music takes you there. Even if you just hit a gong and listen to it fade into silence, the receding sound takes you home.

As The Man said, "The eternal is not touched by what is here." So we struggle with all our daily problems and challenges, but there's something indefinable inside us that redeems us from all the chaos. Of course, we can't quite nail it down, because it's a "shadow reflex," and even if we could, we'd be doing it in time. That isn't the eternal center.

Robert Bly stayed at my house the night before Joe's memorial. We drove over to the church in Santa Monica, and I told Robert the dream I had the night before:

> I dreamt that Joe was holding his hands up like those tomb guardians, ya know, one hand saying, "Come forward, please come forward," and the other saying, "Stay right there . . . don't come any further." And then I got the feeling that Campbell was very excited to see what was on the other side of the great change to come . . . full of anticipation.

Robert said that I should tell that dream at the memorial, and I agreed.

When we got there, Joe's wife, Jean, said that her husband had complained of pains the night of the film premiere. He passed just two weeks later. Her statement shook me, and I took a hit of the little flask of Glenlivet, Campbell's favorite drink, which I'd brought for my talk. I toasted him during my talk, as planned, but then forgot to tell the dream. Scotch is not my drink—it's a little too strong—and it hit me quick. Either that or I was feeling rather emotional and spaced out on my intentions. Reflecting back, though, the dream certainly affirmed that a man who spent his whole life studying "the gods" would be quite pleased to have his curiosity satisfied and his questions answered.

Most of the ancient temples in the world that have survived show an exterior with demons and dragons on the outside, guarding the interior. True spirituality isn't for the faint of heart. You have to look squarely at your inner demons to find some peace. I envision Joseph Campbell permanently in residence now, sitting at the Last Supper, having quite a conversation.

Chapter Seventeen

Peggy Feury
The Method

Actors' bodies are their instruments.

njelica Huston thanked her "guardian angel, Peggy Feury," when she received the Best Actress Award for *Prizzi's Honor* at the Oscars ceremony. Lily Tomlin also thanked Peggy at another ceremony at the Kennedy Center. Who was this woman behind Sean Penn, Laura Dern, Michelle Pfeiffer, Jeff Goldblum, Annette O'Toole, Tina Turner, and me? There almost isn't an actor you can name who *didn't* study with Peggy.

And what does acting have to do with music, John? Well, I studied with Peggy for a couple of years, and a couple of times I managed to do some good acting work. When that happened, she said, "John, you see what you bring from music? Your knowledge of improvisation makes you quickly understand acting."

123

I say this not to toot my own horn but to illuminate the parallels between the arts. In the previous chapter, I spoke of the similarities between music and writing. Acting hooks right up with these two art forms. To keep a live acting performance fresh through repeated performances, the actor changes the phrasing of the lines. That's rhythm. He or she might also change the tempo of the reading. That's almost like singing.

I stumbled into Peggy Feury's acting class after the Doors' big peak. A peak so steep that many who make it to the top slide down the other side quickly due to drug or alcohol abuse. The air is thin up there, and the road back down can be negotiated slowly if one zigzags. I zagged into acting and found that doing a scene on a small stage for twelve people instead of twenty-four thousand at Madison Square Garden caused more stage fright.

I decided that working through that stage fright would be good for me, and would help keep me out of trouble. With The Doors, if Jim was in good shape (as in not too loaded), my confidence had been fairly high, but I didn't have my security blanket (my drums) when I acted. My heart would pound so loud in my chest that I thought I wouldn't be able to hear my acting partner.

"Actors' bodies are their instruments," my new guru said. Peggy herself, according to Angelica Huston, had "a very beautiful figure, quite small and delicate. She had that halfway-to-heaven look: pale eyes and light hair, she liked pale stockings and pearls, and sometimes she looked very angelic." Sometimes she looked very spaced out too.

Narcolepsy is a disease that inhibits the brain's ability to regulate sleep-wake cycles, and therein lay part of Peggy's genius. Unfortunately, the disease also took her life. After she passed, I realized that it could have also taken mine. Sometimes I would meet Peggy at the bottom of Topanga Canyon and hitch a ride with her down the Pacific Coast Highway when she was driving into Hollywood to teach class. I certainly knew she had narcolepsy, but didn't really think through the danger of riding with her if she fell asleep while driving. I should have sung the Doors' lyric: "Keep your eyes on the road, and your hands upon the wheel."

Her weird disease also gave her a gift. You'd be working your ass off, saying your lines and trying to stay in the moment, and there would be Peggy, over on the side nodding out, her head dipping, looking like she was about to fall on the floor. Then, when the acting scene was over, she'd snap out of her trance and critique the work with an incredible eye. She didn't miss a thing. Maybe, while in the alpha state, she saw things the rest of us didn't. The former director of the Lee Strasberg Institute was extremely gifted.

Anjelica again: "She had a way of commenting on a scene that was never destructive, even if you knew she thought it was pretty terrible." Peggy's critique would usually be short when you were good, but when you were off, she would go on for quite a while. Never with malice, though. As Anjelica reflected, "She would tell a story that was always instructive to what you were doing." I even cut my hair for a scene. Peggy had said that musicians are "internal," that they hide behind their music. Actors are "out," she said, then suggested that maybe I should get my hair out of my face. For Ms. Feury, yes; for my dad, years before, no.

I find actors courageous for transforming their bodies into their character by changing their hair, their body weight, the way they walk, the way they talk; they tweak every aspect of their physical self so as to occupy someone else's body. Jack Nicholson said that bringing the character home each night after a shoot is like bad typing, but on the other hand, Angelica said that when they were living together, it felt rather odd to be around him after *The Shining* shoots. Who wouldn't feel that way in the company of someone trying to emulate such a weird, tortured human being?

Unless you're playing someone very glamorous, you have to put aside that part of the ego requiring you to always "look good." And then there's "the truth," which comes through, even with all the makeup, if the actor has talent. Same thing with music. You need to bring enough technique to your instrument to get across your uniqueness, and then the truth comes through. If it's all technique, it's too slick. Peggy was always looking for the truth in each of her students.

The couple of times I understood the parallel between acting and music, say in a scene from a Harold Pinter play, I felt totally free within the character I was playing, and it felt like improvising the right drum fill behind Jim Morrison. Pinter's words were the chord changes I was following as my framework.

One reason why the Traylors (Peggy was married to Bill) finally moved to Bel Air was to cut down the long drive to their acting studio. Unfortunately, a few months after the move, Peggy, driving alone, fell asleep at the wheel. Besides herself, she almost took out the driver in another car. She shouldn't have been driving.

Her memorial at the Mark Taper Forum downtown was full of weeping famous celebs. When Sean Penn spoke, he said he was more nervous than when he saw his wife (Madonna) in hot pants. Some thought the comment tacky, but in my opinion, occasions like that one need humor. Laura Dern reminisced very touchingly about living close to Peggy in Malibu, then starting acting classes and realizing how talented her neighbor was.

After Peggy passed, I immediately went over to the Traylors' house to pay my respects. Jack Nicholson was leaving as I walked up the drive. He had done a movie with Peggy's husband Bill, and I gave him a nod of camaraderie as I silently passed. I gave Bill a big hug, and he tearfully told me a beautiful story.

When they were in China, Peggy had gotten up early one morning and left the hotel. She was gone quite a while, and he started to worry. Then he opened the curtains and looked out the window onto the park. Down below Bill saw hundreds of Chinese doing Tai Chi. Among them was Peggy, waving her arms and moving her legs, trying to imitate her new fellow citizens.

How could you not love this woman who was always looking for the humanity in an actor's performance? There she was, down in the park, living it.

Chapter Eighteen
Robert Bly
Poetic Father Figure

Poetry is the grandfather beat of language.

I n Native American cultures, the wise elders know that without the steady, simple groove of the big drum, none of the flashy, youth-driven polyrhythms on top will mean anything. No steady heartbeat, no resonance. Poets everywhere search for the skeleton of language, the backbone of our verbal communication. Suicide rates among them are high, because good poetry comes directly from the heart. It's scary to be *that* open. The same could be said of my old lead singer, the only difference being that Jim Morrison took the road of slow suicide, via alcohol.

I was greatly fed when I met Robert Bly, whose spirit at the time of this writing is still pushing the envelope in his nineties. Bly offered an alternative to Morrison, whom even my young psyche knew to avoid when his drinking got excessive. I went to one of those early men's groups that Robert ran, and it was just the ticket after losing Jim and two marriages.

Before attending one of the men's group conferences, I had categorized poetry as being all about flowers, but when Robert read his poems and exposed us to other poets, I realized that poetry is direct contact with the soul. It was also very healing to hang out with just my gender for a week. Many of the men at these conferences were making their first attempt to share their feelings, with the stipulation that there would be no dissing of women. I was not the only one who found it helpful to gather occasionally only with other men to share our common experience.

In the '80s, Robert spoke of the male quest in a very popular interview with Keith Thompson. He gave a little history lesson.

"The '50s male," who was hard-working, responsible, fairly well disciplined: he didn't see women's souls very well, though he looked at their bodies a lot. The '50s male was vulnerable to collective opinion: if you were a man, you were supposed to like football games, be aggressive, stick up for the United States, never cry, and always provide. But this image of the male lacked feminine space. It lacked some sense of flow; it lacked compassion in a way that led directly to the unbalanced pursuit of the Vietnam War, just as the lack of feminine space inside Ronald Reagan's head has led to his callousness and brutality toward the poor in El Salvador, toward old people here, the unemployed, schoolchildren, and the poor in general. The '50s male had a clear vision of what a male is, but the vision involved massive inadequacies and flaws.

Then during the '60s, another sort of male appeared. The waste and anguish of the Vietnam War made men question what an adult male really is. And the women's movement encouraged men to actually look at women, forcing them to become conscious of certain things that the '50s male tended to avoid. As men began to look at women and their concerns, some men began to see their feminine side and pay attention to it.

Now, there's something wonderful about all this—the step of the male bringing forth his own feminine consciousness is an important one—and yet I have the sense there is something still missing. Sometimes when I look out at my audiences, perhaps half the young males are what I'd call soft. They're lovely, valuable people and I like them, and they're not interested in harming the earth, or starting wars, or working for corporations. There's something favorable toward life in their whole general mood and style of living. But something's wrong. Many of these men are unhappy. There's not much energy in them.

Some energetic women chose soft men to be their lovers—and in a way, perhaps, their sons. These changes didn't happen by accident. Young men for various reasons wanted harder women, and women began to desire softer men. It seems like a nice arrangement, but it isn't working out. Recently I taught a conference for men only. Each morning I talked about certain fairy tales relating to men's growth, and about the Greek gods that embody what the Greeks considered different kinds of male energy. Often the younger males would begin to talk and within five minutes they would be weeping. The amount of grief and anguish in the younger males was astonishing. The river was deep.

Part of the grief was remoteness from their fathers, which they felt keenly, but part, too, came from the trouble in their marriages or relationships. They had learned to be receptive, and it wasn't enough to carry their marriages. In every relationship, something fierce is needed once in a while: both the man and the woman need to have it. In *The Odyssey*, Hermes instructs Odysseus, when he is approaching a kind of matriarchal figure, that he is to lift and show Circe his sword. It was difficult for many of the younger males to distinguish between showing the sword and hurting someone. They had learned so well not to hurt anyone that they couldn't even lift the sword, even to catch the light of the sun on it! Showing a sword doesn't mean fighting; there's something joyful in it.

Bly went on to say that what men really need is a connection to their "deep masculine," not the shallow masculine of the macho male. "Men already know enough about brute strength, but a deep internal male energy which isn't accessed by gentle Jesus or a guru is needed. It's inside the male psyche. It's forceful action undertaken not without compassion, but with resolve."

Native Americans speak of Mother Earth and Father Sky, and it is in a similar way that I think of Robert Bly as a poetic father figure. When he began his men's groups, he had an intuitive finger on the pulse of the archetypal energy that was bubbling under males all over the world. In a few years, that energy would explode into worldwide consciousness via Robert's hugely successful best seller *Iron John*.

I related when Robert spoke of young men like me. We had grown our hair long and integrated feminine values into our psyches, but we also felt that the modern economy had taken our fathers away from a shoulder-to-shoulder relationship with us, as fathers once had with their sons while doing work on the farm or in the carpentry shop. Now fathers were stuck in office buildings, where their sons couldn't see them or be with them, making it hard to understand that they were shuffling papers to make a living.

The sadness also came from men being forced by the old patriarchal model to stiff-upper-lip it. Robert's men's groups were a place where we could show our vulnerability. He encouraged us to do so by sharing personal stories from his own life. Marion Woodman, a Canadian mythopoetic author and Jungian analyst who trained at the C. G. Jung Institute in Zürich, said of Bly: "With his say-it-like-it-is, gutsy, and sensitive voice, he constellates the king, the warrior, the child, the trickster."

Robert embodied *all* the emotions, and that validated my patchwork of interior feelings, which due to the culture didn't have a voice. He used old fairy tales, which were full of a variety of characters, to emphasize the diversity of our feelings. It was kind of like hearing a symphony containing all the sounds that evoke the entire range of human emotions. One of his most famous poems in the 1980s, "Fifty Males Sitting Together," spoke of youthful estrangement and finding solace in the men's gatherings out in the woods:

He turns away, loses courage, goes outdoors to feed with wild
things, lives among dens and huts, eats distance and silence;
He grows long wings, enters the spiral, ascends.

In his youth, Bly went to Harvard, as did his fellow poets and writers Donald Hall, Will Morgan, Adrienne Rich, Kenneth Koch, Frank O'Hara, John Ashbery, Harold Brodkey, George Plimpton, and John Hawkes. He got a Fulbright grant and went to Norway to translate Norwegian poets. Then he discovered many more poets from India, Spain, South America, and Persia and worked to publish them in the United States, where they were unknown. In the sixties, with the "conflict" in Southeast Asia escalating, Bly won the National Book Award for his poetry collection *The Light around the Body*, which contained strongly antiwar poems.

I had heard of the outrageous speech he delivered when accepting the National Book Award: Bly condemned the Vietnam War, called a draft resister up onstage, and gave him the award money. I too had gone through some early struggles to avoid being drafted, and that speech only endeared him to me further. David Ignatow, winner of the Bollinger Prize for Poetry, described the moment:

> To Robert, at first, the idea of accepting a prize in the middle of a war of devastation upon innocent people was obscene and a travesty of the high purpose of poetry itself. He was for rejecting the prize outright with a written, scathing denunciation, but decided to accept the award on the condition that he be allowed to speak as he wished. It was an unusual request to make since it was the custom to simply accept the prize with a short but graceful thank you and depart from the stage. The speech was written among us fellow poets just hours before the ceremony, and it was an amazing moment in the hall when Robert, after quietly receiving the check, turned to the audience with

his speech in hand and began to read it in his measured but angry voice. We had been forewarned that there would be FBI agents in the audience. He denounced the war, he denounced the writers in the audience who had been sitting idly by, letting the war take its frightful course without a word of protest or expression of conscience, and, finally, he denounced the publishers themselves who had contributed toward prize money and his own publisher in particular for its silence.

Boy, did this moment remind me of when Jim said "Fuck you!" to the rest of the band because we were considering letting one of our songs be used for a car commercial. As Bob Dylan said, "Money doesn't talk, it swears." Back to David Ignatow:

A hush fell upon the auditorium as he called out the name of the representative of the War Resisters League, gave him the check, and urged him to refuse to register for the draft. Open encouragement was tantamount to a violation of a law that had recently passed in Congress. As we looked around, we became aware that about ten men dressed in dark suits rose up from their seats in different parts of the hall . . . then the plain clothes-men walked out all together.

Galway Kinnell, the future Pulitzer Prize winner, was afraid that Robert would be arrested on the spot. Ignatow continued:

As an uproar of talk mixed with boos and cheers broke out in the audience, I, too, was apprehensive that the worst was yet to come, but for now we had won the day and put on notice the government and this distinguished audience, composed of most of the major literary figures of the day and their publishers, that this war could not be suppressed in our thoughts, not in our lives, but had to be met honestly and with conscience.

I wouldn't let fear override the exhilaration—that victory of spirit that swept through us who had helped Robert with his speech. It meant a complete and overwhelming affirmation and vindication of all that Robert stood for as a crusading, visionary figure in the literary world and in the politics of the nation. He had endured insults, threats, and condemnation to make his stand before the artistic and intellectual elite at the full height of his career and poetic talents. He had done it with all the style, gusto, and political passion on the highest level. It was Robert's finest hour, and we who were attached to him through admiration, faith, and common goals were affirmed through him and made to feel our significance before the world.

I'm thinking of Jim again, how he confronted his bandmates because he couldn't make a corporate deal that would compromise our creation. Bly would have many more such moments in the literary world. As the unofficial Father of the Men's Movement, he spawned change that would eventually inspire the Million Man March on Washington.

At the early men's conferences, Robert welcomed everyone, thanked us for coming, and remarked that it took courage to go into the woods with a bunch of men. Normally we were programmed to be competitive and not share our inner feelings. By the end of the week, there was so much camaraderie among us that no one wanted to go back to the real world.

"Honoring Robert Bly is honoring masculinity in myself," said Marion Woodman, one of the most widely read authors on feminine psychology. She continued: "It is honoring masculinity in countless men and women who have touched that lost part of themselves through his conferences and books." The implication here was that men can be strong like Zeus, but benevolent as well.

I now see a similar sadness in recent generations, many of whom remind me of males of the 1980s. The patriarchy is still lying to the youth about war. We hated the draft because it was dragging young men off to an unjust war, but now I think it would be better to bring back the draft, so long as it applies to everyone regardless of socioeconomic background. And I say that as someone with a son of draftable age. Regardless of whether our recent wars are just or not, poor people and minorities are the prime recruiting targets for the military.

It seems like everyone under the age of sixty now has a tattoo (me included), but the old ritual of getting one from an elder as an initiation, after a series of physical tests, is long gone. Some folks are now covering half their bodies with the ink, desperately trying to initiate themselves. Don't get me wrong: I'm not dissing these people. After all, these are *my* people. I feel comfortable around them. But accumulation of more and more tats seems to me emblematic of an attempt to make up for the absence of an honorable elder, someone to dole out tats to them sporadically for their achievements.

So our brave young men (and women!) look like warriors, but haven't been prepared for taking another's life for sometimes vague and questionable reasons. Perhaps it's no coincidence that suicide rates are now extremely high among military personnel, reflecting the damage being done to the psyches of today's youth. And the supposed leaders continue to co-opt our precious rock 'n' roll to do their bidding. Jackson Browne had to sue John McCain for using one of his songs as a theme for his 2008 presidential campaign, and Neil Young criticized Donald Trump for the same sneaky move in 2016.

Naive as it might sound, the twenty-first century needs a powerful nation with a Minister of Peace, alongside a Minister of the Economy, to tap the knowledge of the experts on the subject of peace (Martin Luther King, Gandhi, the Dalai Lama) in governing the nation. More people have died in wars in the last century than ever before in the history of mankind. We are headed toward a cliff, and if we don't try to veer off in the direction of nonviolence, we'll fall right off it.

It's like the two characters in Stewart Stern's brilliant *Rebel Without a Cause* playing "chicken": each of them races toward a steep cliff in an old car, and the first one to jump out is a chicken in the eyes of the onlookers. The screenwriter said that this scene (which I have framed and autographed on my wall) is the most important in the movie. Jim, the James Dean character, is listening to his rival about how not to get his jacket caught on the door handle. "Jump out. No—quick, man! You got to break quick." Looking down at the sheer one-hundred-foot drop to the highway below, they share a cigarette.

BUZZ (*quietly*): This is the edge, boy. This is the end.

JIM: Yeah.

BUZZ: I like you, you know?

JIM: Buzz? What are we doing this for?

BUZZ (*still quiet*): We got to do *something*. Don't we?

Plato, played by Sal Mineo, watches from a distance, thinking that the two rivals look like close friends.

In showing his sword to the literary circle at the National Book Awards, Robert Bly showed us that we are all fellow human beings and that the killing must stop. The thirteenth-century Sufi mystic Rumi has the answer (translation by Coleman Barks):

> Today, like every other day,
> we wake up empty and frightened.
> Don't open the door to the study and begin reading.
> Take down a musical instrument.
> Let the beauty we love be what we do.
> There are hundreds of ways to kneel and kiss the ground.

Music and poetry are two of the very few salves that can quell our warlike spirit. They also teach us tolerance. Hearing Bly, one of the great translators of the twentieth century, read his interpretations of Federico García Lorca, Juan Ramón Jimenez, Pablo Neruda, César Vallejo, Antonio Machado, Tomas Tranströmer, Mirabai, Kabir, and Rainer Maria Rilke is like mainlining many world cultures. I heard Latin music between the lines when I read Bly's translations of Neruda and Machado, I hear Ravi Shankar between the lines of his interpretations of Kabir, and there's a little bit of Beethoven weaving around Robert's translations of Rilke.

When a poem is read by someone who understands it, its meaning is instantly revealed to the listener. "The community flowers when the poem is spoken in the ancient way—that is, with full sound, with conviction, and with the knowledge that the emotions are not private to the person speaking them," Bly once said. This is where the music comes in. Robert has accompanied himself on dulcimer and balalaika, primarily to create a background drone sound for his lines to float on top of. That's where he improvises with phrasing, pauses, and dynamics. Just like a singer would do.

That's also how I drum. It wasn't long before I asked Robert if I could accompany him on a poem or two. I had chosen his "Night Frogs" because I heard things in that poem, just as I heard things in Jim Morrison's lyrics. The first stanza talks of a train hurtling through lonely Louisiana at night. I chose a 3/4 groove, which elicits a loping N'awlins feel. In the second stanza, a woman whispers that one should speak truths. Definitely get soft in this section (pianissimo). Next: "A shape flat and four feet long slips under the door / And lies exhausted on the floor in the morning." Time to squeeze the drumhead with my elbow and tap on it with the other hand, which sounds like someone—or, to be more precise, an animal—talking (I used a calf-skin head for this).

Then I did something I knew would surprise Robert. The fourth stanza is about looking back and seeing a blind spot in the car. "What is it in my father I keep not noticing?" He goes on about not remembering years of his childhood, some parts he can't find now. I started to stagger the 3/4 groove, as if I couldn't play it well. Sort of like an earthquake sporadically interrupting my playing.

Robert quickly glanced at me and noticed that I was still rocking my head, playing the groove. The staggered groove was internal, so Bly knew I meant for him to continue reading at his rhythmic pace as I staggered the groove to match the music to the text. I didn't want to spoil the impact by telling him ahead of time that I was going to do this. It made him stagger the lines a little too, as if he were stuttering. In the last section, I started the steady groove again, softly, building it, and then added a ritard to the ending, slowing it down to a stop to give the effect of a train coming into the station, as Robert spoke the last line: "Night frogs give out the croak of the planet turning."

Judging from the audience's response, it went very well. When we talked afterward, Robert said, "I couldn't believe you did that! That you stopped playing . . . and started again!" The smile on his face said that it had worked.

Many conferences later, in which Robert had ranted and cajoled stories and poetry from inside of a very colorful serape, complete with tapping on a Tibetan drum, his antics continued to feed my psyche. Sometimes he looked like a cross between Vallejo and a Rinpoche pulling masks from behind his back to dramatize his telling of Grimms' fairy tales. It was riveting.

I worked up an accompaniment to Bly's translation of Rilke's "The Man Watching." We did it at a benefit for the Joseph Campbell archives in Santa Barbara, California. Robert introduced me to the two thousand people crammed into the Arlington Theatre and said that he loved having me accompany him because he never knew what I was going to do! The audience was already primed by the competition between our two books as they climbed the *New York Times* best-seller list. *Riders on the Storm* was number three, and *Iron John*—described by the *Times* as "Important . . . Powerful . . . Timely"—would stay at number one on the charts for an unheard-of sixty-two weeks. The *Santa Barbara Independent* described our performance at the Arlington as "that Nouveau Pagan Pantheist Sprite," and we raised a bunch of dough for the archives of one of Robert's mentors.

Bly's voracious appetite for new ideas was catching and helped me understand Jim Morrison better. Besides introducing me to the works of Campbell, Robert turned me on to Jung and his sidekick James Hillman. An incredible literary lineage was coming down my chute, and like Bly, I found my appetite for new ideas and insights growing. In reaction to the women's movement, new sensitive males were now acquiring a fierceness. It was a fierceness like Robert's when he threw down an academic translation of the Persian poet Rumi on a table in front of Coleman Barks, a poet and scholar from Georgia, and said: "These poems are in prison . . . release them!" That lit a fire under Barks, and he went on to become the foremost translator of the most popular poet in America (though a lot of Americans didn't know that their country bombed near Rumi's homeland when it bombed Afghanistan).

Robert Bly loves creativity, and his incredible, intuitive, generous soul nurtures that same love in others. He introduced me to an Iranian musician, Reza Derakshani, and we started playing music together, eventually performing at the Kennedy Center in Washington, DC. Reza would always ask the audience to hold their applause, to keep their energy "inside." The effect was very powerful. Bly also invited his sidekick at the men's conferences, the mythologist Michael Meade, and the author James Hillman to collaborate on what turned out to be a very successful anthology of poetry for men called *The Rag and Bone Shop of the Heart*.

The comparatively shy but supremely talented Galway Kinnell reflected on his friend:

> Robert spoke with absolute conviction about everything and I was sure he would be an unbudgeable dogmatist. On the contrary, it turned out he was more drawn to new truth, even somebody else's, than attached to old, even his own; and in the middle of a conversation he could be charmed and won over by an idea directly contradicting the idea he had just been expounding.

That's why, when introducing Bly at a poetry reading in Los Angeles, I said: "Robert Bly is a mensch. He says that 25 to 40 percent of what he says is BS. (It's nice to know what's up ahead!) Robert Bly is a real man." Real in the sense that he has strong convictions but is open to being challenged. Paul Feroe, the publisher of one of Robert's books, sums up the feeling at a Bly reading:

> You see the enthusiasm and ideas flying between the stage and the audience . . . it's incredible. All around, people are out of their seats with ideas, they are lined three deep at microphones to share or shout their insights, and for most this exchange of energy can't go on long enough. Robert has that effect on people.

A truly remarkable musician, poet, and magician. A mensch.

Chapter Nineteen

Barbara Morrison

Soul Sister

Playing the Blue Note . . . and playing it well.

"You haven't been in the 'hood much, have you!" she joked.

"What does that mean? I've been to Lemert Park many, many times!" I said defensively. "I paid for the sound system at the World Stage!" That was an arts venue founded by the great jazz drummer Billy Higgins.

She clobbered me with the punch line. "We call it black ass, please, not black-eyed peas!"

I almost hit the floor of Delicious, the restaurant where we were having lunch, but regained my composure in time to choose my sides. "Uh . . . I'll have collard greens, black ass peas, and smothered chicken."

Since I was with the neighborhood's unofficial mayor (everyone in the area knows and loves Barbara Morrison), the African American woman taking the order didn't rip my head off for that comment. She just chuckled with Barbara like they were sharing an inside joke on the honky. Then I remembered that recently my doc had said to cut the fat out of my diet. *Fuck it*, I thought, rationalizing that I was with someone who reeked of soul and having a heart attack right then and there would be all right.

My health karma was nothing compared to this beautiful sixty-five-year-old black woman who, like Aretha and Janis Joplin, could give you goose bumps just by singing one note. As we sat there, more folks came by, all of them friendly. This was after the infamous shooting in Ferguson, Missouri, in 2014, but since I was on a lunch date with "the Queen," dudes with dreads down to their waist were patting me on the back and putting out a strong love vibe.

I stumbled into a second-half-of-life friendship with this soul sister when she sang with a band at the surprise party for my fiftieth birthday. "Hi! I'm Jim's sister, Barbara Morrison . . . great to meet you! Wanna sit in?" That's the kind of humor she'd shoot out of both sides of her extremely talented mouth. That mouth is connected to a three-and-a-half-octave vocal range that trumped all the other singers at the Hollywood Bowl tribute to Sarah Vaughan.

As a young singer trying to break into the music business, Barbara understood that it would be tough, so she looked up Sammy Davis Jr.'s number in the phone book and called him (hard to imagine, but true). He picked up the phone (imagine *that!*), said no, he couldn't help her, but he knew of a guy who managed singers, a Mr. Brown. Barbara called Mr. Brown, and lo and behold, it was the master jazz bassist Ray Brown, who was managing Ella Fitzgerald among others! He told Barbara, "Call me in ten years . . . you need to pay some dues."

He was very surprised when Barbara called him ten years later—but then he said maybe she should wait *another* ten! Well, the never-give-up Ms. Morrison started working gigs with Ernie Andrews and James Moody and went on the road with Ray Charles.

At one gig she recognized the legendary songwriter Carole King wandering around backstage. "Where are the Raelettes?" King asked. "I'd like to meet them."

"Is your name Carole?"

"Yes."

"Carole King?"

"Yes."

"You're talkin' to one of them right now! Come with me."

Later Barbara said that the other singers didn't know Carole King had penned Aretha's biggest hit, "Natural Woman." Barbara Morrison is a walking encyclopedia of music. She knows everything and everybody.

She sang with Jimmy Smith, Dizzy Gillespie, Count Basie, Joe Williams, Kenny Burrell, Ron Carter, Etta James, Dr. John, Johnny Otis, and Tony Bennett. Ten more years passed, and she continued performing, singing with Gerald Wilson, Esther Phillips, Terence Blanchard, Mel Torme, Nancy Wilson, Joe Sample, Keb' Mo', Stevie Wonder, Dianne Reeves, Chaka Khan, Dionne Warwick, and Lou Rawls.

Then she called Ray Brown again. This time he said, "Come to New York. You're playing with me at the Blue Note." The Blue Note was a legendary jazz club in New York City. Well, Barbara was gigging in Sweden, thinking that she could head directly to the Big Apple, then return home to LA after that. A few days later, she flipped on the boob tube, put on CNN because it was the only English-language channel on Swedish TV, and flopped onto the bed. Then she noticed the chyron scrolling across the bottom of the TV screen: "Great jazz bassist Ray Brown dies in his sleep." Talk about playing the blue note. She had to live it.

Barbara Morrison certainly had paid enough other dues to sing the blue note, including, as I mentioned earlier, some tough health dues. After she got on the bus one day and immediately passed out, she was taken to the hospital, where the doctor said, "Haven't you been taking your shots?" She hadn't had a clue that she had diabetes. It was diagnosed so late that Barbara had to have not one but both of her feet removed.

When I took her out to lunch that day at Delicious, I asked her if she could walk. She got up and started dancing. She was about to get new prostheses, she told me, so if anybody gave her any shit, they'd get whacked with some pretty strong legs.

Barbara Morrison is one of the best examples in the world of the triumph of spirit over matter. She embodies the idea that we are more than flesh and bones. We are sound, and all of it is music to her. She eats and drinks music, running her performing arts center and singing her ass off wherever they will have her, and we are blessed to hear it.

Chapter Twenty

His Holiness the Dalai Lama

Zen Slap

Don't follow leaders, watch your parking meters.

I made a mistake when I met the Dalai Lama, and he gave me what I deserved for what I did. But we need to go back a ways.

I had been an admirer of the Dalai Lama for many years, so I was interested when I noticed a benefit for the Tibetan Foundation at the Beverly Wilshire Hotel featuring His Holiness. It cost a few hundred dollars a ticket, which got you a dinner in a huge auditorium, with the Dalai Lama sitting way up onstage at a table with the movie stars. If you paid $500, you'd get dinner *and* a personal *darshan* from "The Man." In Hinduism, a darshan is a "blessing from the guru." I signed up.

At the reception, there was a large private room for those of us who had anted up the bigger bucks. Entering, I got in a long line of about two hundred fellow devotees who were waiting for their personal moment. I could see the bespectacled monk at the front of the line, with his red and orange robes draped over one shoulder. On one side of the guru was Harrison Ford, and Richard Gere was on the other side. It was interesting that as I got closer, my emotions began to surface. Was it projection, or was the Dalai Lama causing this to happen? Didn't matter. It felt very cleansing to have my tear ducts opened.

Harrison Ford had been enrolled in the UCLA acting program when my old bandmates were in film school. They had enlisted him to be a grip (technical helper) with the crew that shot us at the Hollywood Bowl, so we had met before. Back then, he was an excellent carpenter who helped with the sets for our gig. As I reached him, I reintroduced myself, and we reminisced about Paul Rothchild, our old record producer. Paul had recently passed, and I knew Harrison was buds with him. "Ya know, chain-smoking weed took him out," I said. Harrison joked, "Yeah . . . I better back off!" We smiled at each other, and then I approached the famous mystic.

He put a white scarf around my neck, which was the tradition, and then it happened. Like Jim when he met my old guru Maharishi, I had this impulse to look deeply into the Dalai Lama's eyes, deep enough to be intrusive. I gave in to the impulse because I knew he had some truth, but I went too far.

My eyes might as well have said to his eyes, *Prove it, prove you're as amazing as your rep.* It was then that the Zen slap came.

The Dalai Lama knew I was overstepping my bounds—or his bounds—by glaring into the windows into his soul. He quickly reached out his hand to take mine and, I thought, to shake it, but instead he used the handshake to *push* me, shoving me over to Richard Gere. I cordially shook Gere's hand and moved on out of the way.

Michael Stipe, lead singer for the rock group REM, was on the side, and I struck up a conversation with him. He said the Dalai Lama was hurrying all these people through because he was tired. Even hearing that, I was still feeling rather emotional. What had that all been about? I felt that I got my karma for overstepping my bounds, and something in me was very thankful about the way he treated me. It was so unexpected because I had put him up on a pedestal.

Can you imagine what it's like for a public figure like a spiritual leader to have all these strangers wanting to meet you? I can. I've experienced Doors fans being gaga to meet yours truly, and sometimes it has felt weird. Public personalities certainly don't have all the answers, as projected upon them. As I wrote in my first memoir, we have to go to the bathroom, and get divorced, just like everyone else. So something in me appreciated being "put in my place" by the Dalai Lama.

For some reason, I remained teary-eyed throughout the whole dinner after the private VIP darshan. Back in the '60s, when I was hanging out with Maharishi, the vibe was one of profound beauty—"all you need is love" was the feeling. The sentiments that came up at the Tibetan dinner seemed to have more to do with my interior. As George Harrison wrote in "Pisces Fish":

> There's a temple on an island
> I think of all the Gods and what they feel
> You can only find them in the deepest silence
> I got to get off of this big wheel

I'm not facing "the big C" (cancer), as the transcendental "quiet" Beatle had to do, so I don't feel quite the urgent need to get off the karmic wheel. But at my age the big S (as in silence) is not too far around the corner, and what is silence . . . but music! "The music is not in the notes, but in the silence between," so said Mozart. Everyone has an internal symphony playing, and if Coleman Barks, Rumi's great translator, is right that the microcosm is *bigger* than the macrocosm, then we've all got a musical extravaganza going on in our mind that we can tap into at will.

Once again, the Indian holy man who opened the Woodstock Music Festival, Sri Swami Satchidananda, nails it:

> And if you all join wholeheartedly (500,000 music fans), after the chant we are going to have at least one whole minute of absolute silence. Not even the cameras will click at that time. And in that silent period, that one minute of silence, you are going to feel the great, great power of that sound and the wonderful peace that it can bring in you and into the whole world.

The Dalai Lama is a virtuoso at exploring the sounds of that silence.

Not wanting to step on any creature, not even an ant, he also epitomizes nonviolence in a very violent world. The Dalai Lama's life very dramatically demonstrates holding the opposites. That's why I hear his song so loud and clear. Everyone's path is a song played out over a lifetime. Rumi gets it:

> [Give] more of your life to this listening . . .
>   . . . so you are to
>   the one who talks to the deep ear in
>   your chest. I should sell my tongue
>   and buy a thousand ears when that
>   One steps near and begins to speak.

Whether your song is a mellow ballad or a hot salsa perfect for partying 24/7, the point is to listen to it, then play it fully, with compassion.

The Dalai Lama's official title is "the Incarnation of Compassion." Compared to all of us running around frantically, his center is certainly a breath of fresh air. Now I want all of you readers to stop—because this is the end of the chapter anyway—and take a big, deep breath. Then exhale. Then listen to the silence.

Chapter Twenty-One

Gustavo Dudamel

The Rocker and the Dude

"Juan, Mahler is heavy metal, si?"

T he next person I met who really understands the power of silence was a man who makes his living making sound—a very beautiful sound.

I played the Doors card to get into the green room of the Walt Disney Concert Hall. "Do you think the Maestro would want to meet Jim Morrison's drummer?" I said to security. In response, my girlfriend Ildiko and I were whisked backstage with the film composer Charles Bernstein and his wife. Then we had to wait. And wait.

Based partly on my early exposure to orchestral music, I had a hunch that we were waiting for someone who might be the heir to Leonard Bernstein's legacy, someone who might become the greatest classical music conductor of the twenty-first century. Little did I know that "the Dude"—as in the hotdog named after him at Pink's, the legendary LA hot-dog stand, not as in the Jeff Bridges character in *The Big Lebowski*—was changing from his tuxedo into a polo shirt and slacks, after conducting the Los Angeles Philharmonic in an incredibly powerful performance of *Symphonie Fantastique* by Hector Berlioz.

When we were finally led into the inner sanctum, it was packed with classical music's literati, and Placido Domingo's son introduced himself. The rest of the crowd looked very important, but not as important as the man of the hour, Gustavo Dudamel. He smiled at me, took my hand, and bowed. Then, with his curly dark mop top draped over my wrist, he didn't rise for almost a minute. It was embarrassing. It was also incredibly flattering; his homage was reflective of the range of the young man's musical taste. Six months later, I saw an article on LA's new twenty-seven-year-old conductor in which he said he was well aware of Led Zeppelin, salsa, and jazz.

I had caught Dudamel's interview on *60 Minutes* and was very impressed by his humility. The interviewer tried to get him to acknowledge his new stature as the world's most sought-after conductor, but he just kept saying, "I have much to learn. I have much to learn." I checked out the YouTube video of his performance with the Venezuelan Youth Orchestra and was enthralled. During Leonard Bernstein's "Mambo," he had the musicians standing up and dancing while playing! So I knew before many people did that someone special was on his way from Caracas to "Disneyland."

After he rose from his bow, I proceeded with the script I'd rehearsed in my head. "Gustavo, I didn't come here because of your long hair!"

The entire room roared. Way before rock 'n' rollers let their locks drape over their ears, classical music had been tagged with the moniker "music for longhairs." Some of the rock musicians of the British Invasion during the '60s may have been inspired by the classical lads. The Kinks, the Rolling Stones, and the Zombies certainly looked like Beethoven with their curls dangling over the collars of their sport jackets and ruffled shirts. Now our two genres, classical and rock, were connected. Some stuffed shirts might think connected by the "hair" only, but I was out to prove otherwise. "I played timpani on the Berlioz piece in high school, so I know your world." The Venezuelan wunderkind smiled broadly. He graciously, even enthusiastically, posed for photos with everyone.

The LA Philharmonic's new conductor, Maestro Gustavo Dudamel, is a living example of the results of El Sistema, Venezuela's program of taking impoverished kids and teaching them classical music. His enthusiasm for El Sistema is boundless because he knows that he himself was saved by it and he wants to give back. Gustavo really cares about the kids in the program, as did his late mentor, El Sistema's founder, José Abreu. Abreu once summed up the *milagro* (magic) of El Sistema: "If you put a musical instrument in the hand of a kid, he or she will not pick up a gun."

Even if this is an old idea, it is still somewhat of a miracle that it works. The creative impulse, which resides in everyone, can act as a *curandero* (healer) when it is directed at reimagining the dead-end paths down which poor children are headed, when it is used to point to new roads going in a limitless number of directions. America has been slow to realize the efficacy of this idea. In fact, it's embarrassing that our country, with all its wealth and resources, is always cutting funding for the arts, not expanding it. Especially when we could be finding an antidote for the increased gun violence in the United States by increasing support for fields that foster new imagination. Holding on to our narrow vision that South America stole our name, we know something is happening south of the border, but we "don't know what it is, do we, Mr. Flag Waver?" And it's completely under the CIA's radar.

Moreover, this idea of handing kids instruments to keep them from picking up guns came from a country that one of our previous presidents called a member of the "Axis of Evil." Venezuela certainly has its political troubles, but some Venezuelan officials are doing at least one thing right. They know that art and culture are the glue between peoples. If we can be open to understanding the "other," we just might get along better. Not only is being open to understanding other peoples simply the right thing to do, but this understanding has become widespread in the classical music community around the world.

The great music man Quincy Jones said, "Brahms, Beethoven, Basie, Bo Diddley, and Bird all had to deal with the same fuckin' twelve notes." Out of that chromatic scale came the world's tremendous musical diversity. Maybe Dudamel and El Sistema are right: maybe music *can* save the world. The United States is a big melting pot, the great experiment that has made a home for a greater diversity of cultures than can be found in any other nation. And one way to fast-track all cultures on earth into getting along is to channel the power of the arts.

Music certainly changed my life. As a fourteen-year-old music student in junior high, I saw a sentimental film on Johann Strauss. *Tales from the Vienna Woods* swept me away so much that I was swooning. Mr. Armour, my music teacher, noticed my reaction and told me he was going to screen it again if I wanted to stay. I sat in the empty hall with my teacher, weeping over "The Blue Danube." I was hooked. I'd had no idea yet that music would be the undercurrent of my life. The poet William Stafford captured how that felt in "The Way It is":

> There's a thread you follow. It goes among
> things that change. But it doesn't change.
> People wonder about what you are pursuing.
> You have to explain about the thread.
> But it is hard for others to see.
> While you hold it you can't get lost.
> Tragedies happen; people get hurt
> or die; and you suffer and get old.
> Nothing you do can stop time's unfolding.
> You don't ever let go of the thread.

When Gustavo was a five-year-old kid, he set up his toy figures in a half-circle like an orchestra, with one of them on a cardboard box as the podium, and played classical records. He told his mom not to mess any of it up because he was coming back later to do some more conducting. Putting our two childhood stories side by side, I am by no means saying that I am in the same league as the Maestro. The only comparison is that we both wave our arms a lot and hold sticks.

My second time in the green room was as thrilling as the first. We entered Disney Concert Hall, Frank Gehry's "steel rosebud," and immediately were warmed by the glorious wooden enclave. This auditorium is so inviting that it almost doesn't matter what you hear there. To be inside that room is to be back inside the womb. The Maestro came out to huge applause, and he hadn't conducted a note yet. You could feel the orchestra's admiration for him already. He had cropped his wild hair somewhat and put on a few pounds since my girlfriend and I saw him the year before. Even at the shorter length, his locks seemed uncontainable. Maybe the idea was to corral the hair so it wouldn't compete as much with the arms for control of the orchestra. Still, the curls sort of underscored everything his arms were saying.

The LA Phil's new leader began by conducting with his eyebrows. And his fingertips. Pianissimo. A little kitty kneading the air, then playing with a small mouse. Then the tempo increased, and he did a little sashay from side to side, prancing as if marching in place. Then the demonic rose up for the fortissimo, and his whole body pounced on the orchestra, exacting its prey of sound. I know a couple of members of the orchestra, and they say that, even though he is not the composer, playing in his orchestra feels like your conductor is creating the music in the moment, almost like jazz.

When I heard that the Dude's Simón Bolívar Orchestra (the former Venezuelan Youth Orchestra) was coming to Los Angeles, my anticipation was visceral. I knew that I was about to get a dose of what has healed seven hundred thousand young Venezuelans via El Sistema.

It was culture shock to sit at the Disney Concert Hall in Los Angeles and look down at a hundred twenty-something musicians with jet-black hair and olive-complexioned skin. They ripped into the repertoire of European classical music like there was no tomorrow. The Simón Bolívar Orchestra from Venezuela played the music of two-hundred-year-old dead, white European composers like their lives depended on it, and in some cases it might have. They played with such gusto that the audience immediately jumped out of their seats as if they were at a rock concert, yelling, "Encore! Encore!"

On a recent PBS special about Dudamel, Tavis Smiley asked the correct question and the Maestro gave the correct answer: Was Dudamel playing "dated music"? The ever-present Gustavo replied, "It's not the same . . . we're reinterpreting it!" And reinterpreting it they are. It's as if none of us saw it coming: Beethoven's butt needed a direct shot (mainline) of salsa! The Venezuelans have Latin music coursing through their veins, and even their symphony orchestra will stand up and dance while playing if so moved. The obvious enthusiasm comes from the awareness among most of the musicians that El Sistema is probably their only chance of getting out of the dire environment into which they were born. That's why they practice their asses off.

The shadow side of all this passion is that, as the seasoned players of the LA Phil warn young musicians, pacing yourself makes for a longer career. Like thirty-three-year-old Rafael Nadal, the passionate young Spanish tennis champion, thirty-nine-year-old Dudamel, the gifted young conductor from Caracas, already suffers occasionally from physiological problems. Nadal hits every ball as if it's his last, putting everything possible into it. Dudamel approaches every note of every symphony he's conducting the same way. The tennis player has knee problems; the conductor's shoulder and neck give him occasional trouble. But of course, there is something thrilling about watching someone "go for it" in every moment. The concentration they bring is profound.

I could never have imagined that Gustavo taking over the symphony orchestra would have united an entire city of millions of people only a few years later. The celebration of the one-hundredth anniversary of the Los Angeles Philharmonic, with its young visionary leading the helm, was an incredible day. The streets of LA were blocked to cars and kept open for walkers and cyclists. For eight miles, from the Disney Concert Hall to the Hollywood Bowl, the route was sprinkled with eighteen hundred of the most diverse musicians on the planet. String quartets from the Phil, mariachis from Mexico, brass bands from Central America—all were there to represent the many, many different cultures in the City of Angels and to show that there are no borders around the well of creativity. And leading the parade that day was the Maestro with his wife and son, the three of them riding bikes across town!

So yes, there's a revolution going on, and I'd had a sense that it was coming when I saw the Dude guest-conduct the LA Phil several years before, but I didn't know the extent of it. What this is, and what El Sistema has produced, is a border crossing. When Latino musicians can understand European classical music as well as or *better* than their white European counterparts, a healing occurs. Racism diminishes. Then, if Caucasians can get into salsa . . . if African Americans can appreciate country music . . . if, if, if . . .

So the City of Angels has been blessed. We almost missed capturing the young Turk by one day: the Chicago Symphony was champing at the bit to sign him the day after he committed to LA. It seems right, though, to have him here in LA, where half the population is Hispanic. We won the lottery. My prayer for Gustavo is that he survives the United States, by which I mean that this is a country that builds celebrities up and then knocks them down. I think his humility will keep him grounded.

This line of thought prompted me once to leave the green room with a parting remark. "Gustavo, much has happened to you since we met years ago." He was quickly nodding his head up and down in agreement.

"I have a suggestion, which you've already been doing." His eyes widened.

"Don't forget to breathe!"

The extremely gifted young man let out a huge laugh and said, "Please come back." We will certainly do that, again and again.

Recently, I battled the LA traffic gridlock again, making my way downtown to see the Dude. Gustavo was doing another marathon fest, Mahler this time. He had corralled and prodded the LA Phil into performing all nine of Mahler's symphonies in a couple of weeks! A Herculean feat. Tonight it was the Seventh, and as usual, time seemed to stop when the curly haired Venezuelan picked up the baton. And time literally did stop when, at the end of the last movement, the Maestro swiped the baton, cueing the last note.

Dudamel, like John Cage, understands that "the silences are as important as the sounds." When he finishes conducting a piece, he doesn't put his arms down, but waits until the muse has left the room. He waits longer than any conductor I've ever seen. When his audience has absorbed a lot of sound, as in a forty-five-minute symphony, The Dude knows that a lot of silence is required to balance what just went before. Sometimes he seems to wait for several minutes before freeing us to applaud. The silence is so "loud" that it travels through "pin drop time" and beyond.

I saw Gustavo conduct a modern Hungarian piece that started very quietly. So he told the orchestra that he would conduct two or three bars of silence before the actual piece began, to make sure they came in as subtly, as quietly, as possible. When he did just that, the audience was extra attentive, wondering if they were hearing sound or not. What they were hearing was the counterpart to sound. The experience was magical, like a true group meditation. It was precious to be in that space. I almost didn't want Gustavo to break the spell, but when he finally did, the applause was delicious!

The esteemed *LA Times* classical music critic Mark Swed captured the feeling in the hall during that performance: "Dudamel does not hesitate to let the quietest passages be next to inaudible. By straining to hear, you felt a palpable tension throughout the hall, and the crescendo that would follow, turned overwhelming. Dudamel remained on the podium for a full minute in still meditation. They created a stunned, attentive silence." Out of silence, comes sound. If it's quality sound (doesn't matter if it's a symphony or a rock song), when you arrive back into the silence, it should feel deeper.

After that performance, I made my way to the green room, Gustavo saw me and began shouting, "Juan, Juan!" I said, "El Maestro es poquito loco," and our usual bantering began. (In the green room after an earlier LA Phil performance, he had quickly handed me a shot of vodka, which I downed with a grimace. Another time I spilled a little beer on his Berlioz score, and later he said that every time he opened it to study it, he thought of me!) We did our usual ritual of bowing to each other, showing as much respect as we could muster. He remarked that I would never be able to beat him at this game, because he would grovel all the way to the floor. Upon rising, my friend, and musical idol, said, "Mahler is very heavy metal, sí?" Then he started chanting the main melodic line, and it *did* sound like a lead guitar!

I quickly curtailed my hysterical laughter when he motioned to his left and, glancing over, I saw Julie Andrews out of the corner of my eye. He introduced me, and she continued the conversation they had been having when I came in. She said that she would try to see him conduct in London, he said that would be great, and Julie made her exit. I was disappointed not to have the chance to ask her if she had ever heard John Coltrane's version of "My Favorite Things."

Driving home, I couldn't contain the enthusiasm I'd just received through the medium of sound. I felt giddy, having fully accepted the transference that the Maestro has bestowed on his audience that night. It was as if we had been hooked up to a direct IV of his love for the music and it had filled our veins, pulsing ecstasy through our bodies. That night I understood why people risk their lives to hear music that is so totally connected with their soul.

After seeing my hometown orchestra many more times, something unusual happened. Gustavo himself gave me a call. He said that the LA Phil was doing its yearly fundraising gala concert, that year's theme was "California Soul," and he wanted me to play with them.

I thought of the classical music matrons, I mean patrons, who might turn up their noses at this idea. The Doors had built their foundation on breaking musical barriers. We covered a song from a German opera on our first album (Bertolt Brecht's "Alabama Song"), and we were well aware of the music of Igor Stravinsky, Karlheinz Stockhausen, and Miles Davis. On our second album, we wrote backup for Jim's "Horse Latitudes" poem in the style of *musique concrète*, an avant-garde, electronic, and minimalist concept. Just as world music feeds the Maestro, so it fed a rock band.

The program Gustavo envisioned for the gala concert would open with Jerry Goldsmith's "Love Theme" from the film *Chinatown*, followed by a work by the local minimalist composer John Adams, then something from Frank Zappa, a world premiere from John Adams's student Julia Adolphe, a piece by André Previn, and finally, well, would I play "LA Woman" with the orchestra?

WOW. Inside I was screaming, *Yes!*, but first I asked who would be singing. Chris Martin from Coldplay wants to do it badly, Gustavo replied. Well then! "I'm very interested!" I told him.

I knew the gorgeous theme from *Chinatown*, John Adams had won the Pulitzer for music, Frank Zappa was one of our bandmates when we played the Whisky a Go Go, and I had long salivated over Previn's jazz piano playing before he became the LA Phil's conductor. Would I sit in with eighty-five of the greatest classical musicians in the world? YES!

I started working with the orchestral arranger, David Campbell (Beck's dad!), who had a very impressive résumé and was quite competent. Unfortunately, when I said that I felt that change was needed in a couple of sections, David told me that symphony orchestras are like Broadway shows and both are like giant battleships: difficult to turn around. He'd had to turn in the arrangement a month earlier so that the string players could work on their bowing. Making changes now would cost money, and this was a fundraiser.

As if there wasn't enough pressure playing with perhaps the greatest classical orchestra in the world, I had felt that I had to say something. After all, I had arranged the song with the band. The producers were very kind when I spoke up, though, and said it would be okay. First hurdle passed.

I tried to keep my arms down when walking up to the podium to say something to the orchestra at the first rehearsal. Sweat rings had stained my shirt. "I just want you to know that having you perform one of our songs is an honor, and also, I wanted you to know that I know a bit about your world. I saw Zubin Mehta conduct this orchestra on his first night at the old Philharmonic Auditorium many years ago." All the musicians started stamping their feet (with bows in their hand, that was the only way to applaud).

"I want to fit into your ensemble," I added, "so I'm going to use brushes instead of overpowering you with sticks." More stomping.

The rehearsal went okay, but there were some sound problems to be fixed. I tried to calm myself that night with the mantra "You don't want to peak until opening night." It didn't work. I had a slew of notes for the orchestra, but there wasn't time to relay them the next day. Fortunately, it got better. On the opening night red carpet, I told Gustavo that at the first rehearsal I hadn't been able to hear anything very well. He said it had been the same for him. "But yesterday went better," I said, "and my fears disappeared." The Maestro smiled, as if to say he agreed.

The LA Philharmonic roadies were exceptional. They told me where to stand, when to enter, and where to go. I was about to jump the final hurdle. Before we started, Chris Martin playfully took off his tuxedo jacket, to laughs from the crowd. I was wearing a thrift shop tuxedo jacket with tails and silver angel wings embroidered on the back. After Chris's move, I impulsively turned around and showed the City of Angels how I could fly. The audience roared. We all sat down to begin.

In Dudamel's office a few days before, I had said to the Maestro that in rock bands the drummer usually counts off the tunes.

"Great," he said, "you do that."

"No," I said, "you're the conductor of the greatest orchestra in the world, you should start it." Still, I was worried that if he didn't get the right tempo, the train would have left the station and there would be no turning back pulse-wise.

"Why don't you cue me?" I said. "I'll start the tempo for a couple bars, then you cue in the orchestra?"

He thought that would work great. And it did.

In rehearsal Gustavo had said that, to end the piece, I should be the one to cut it off. The problem was that I was in the back of the orchestra. "Let's do it together," I suggested. "Keep an eye on each other."

"But do your fills, then we'll end together," the Dude added.

So that's what we did. It was a great thrill to cut off eighty-five musicians with a giant cymbal crash, and the audience seemed to love it.

The plan was to do "Good Vibrations" by the Beach Boys for an encore. For that one, 150 singers from the Los Angeles Master Chorale stood behind me. With the chorus in the rear and the orchestra in the front, it was goose-bump time for yours truly with music in stereo surround sound. As I channeled drummer Hal Blaine's parts on the original recording, confetti made out of California patterns dropped from the ceiling and collected around me.

All in all, playing under the baton of one of my new, young sound teachers was a night to remember. My ears were blessed yet again.

I got an even greater thrill backstage in the green room after the performance. I noticed Herbie Hancock in the crowd, took a deep breath, and went up to him. "I've been trackin' you for years and years."

A big smile crept over Herbie's face as he said, "It was great to finally hear you play live!"

I almost turned around to see who he was talking about. But he was talking about me. Now I could RIP. Yet another blessing on my ears.

Chapter Twenty-Two

Paul Simon

Rhymin' Simon

In sound churches such as these,
"we all shall be received."

"I can't believe you remembered that story!" Paul Simon said to me after he performed a miraculous concert at the legendary Ryman Auditorium in Nashville, Tennessee.

Waiting backstage for about half an hour for "The Man" to come out after his show, and getting bored, I started to roam around on the historic main stage. In 1936, Bill Monroe gave birth to bluegrass music here. I could feel the spirit of that era as I clapped my hands to check out the acoustics. The entire hall is made of wood, benches included (there are no seats). The sound was identical to the beautifully resonant Walt Disney

Concert Hall in Los Angeles, which is also made of wood. I had clapped my hands on that stage as well, while waiting to meet Gustavo Dudamel.

Clapping gives a sense of how much echo is in the room. You want some echo, but not too much. Like Frank Gehry's LA masterpiece, the Ryman is perfect acoustically. I could feel the vibe of all the acts that had graced the original Grand Ole Opry's wooden boards, from Minnie Pearl, with her price tag dangling from her hat, to Dolly Parton, Tammy Wynette, Loretta Lynn, Hank Williams, and Patsy Cline. "Historically cool since 1892," the Ryman has attracted modern musicians such as Ringo Starr, Neil Young, and the Foo Fighters.

In sound churches such as these, "we all will be received," as Paul Simon's "Graceland" lyric warmly suggests. Even the ugly history of slavery was etched into the wood paneling along the balcony. Performers could look up to see the "Confederate gallery" permanently pressed into the wall, separating the upper seats from the lower.

That display reminded me of the shit Paul got after the African-tinged *Graceland* album was released. After he enlisted musicians from the Motherland continent to actualize his sonic vision, critics had attacked Simon with the label "cultural colonialist." Lots of critics are frustrated artists who didn't achieve the level they were hoping for, instead they lean heavily on the license to "criticize" they feel comes with the related word "critic." Paul had not only paid his musicians triple scale for their efforts, but he had also elevated the a cappella singing group Ladysmith Black Mambazo to international star status. The African musicians he collaborated with, who were playing with him at the Ryman, love him deeply as a brother.

And now, that evening, Simon's very talented, dark-skinned bass player, Bakithi Kumalo, and the equally gifted Cameroon guitarist Vincent Nguini had courageously faced the racist past of the American South that was written on the walls. The only "rising again" would not be coming from the old Confederacy but through these brave men of sound, song brothers rejoicing together.

The Rock and Roll Hall of Fame's entry on Paul says: "Between the lines, his multi-cultural fusion reinforced the notion that music is a universal language that rises above politics." (His belief in music as a universal language is also why Gustavo Dudamel has been reluctant to get involved in the volatile politics of his native Venezuela. He feels that the experience of playing in an orchestra teaches tolerance.) "Simon also helped open the mass audience's ears to the marvelous forms of music that lay beyond their home borders," the Hall of Fame entry continued. "Paul Simon deserves acclaim for making the world feel a little bit more like a community of kindred spirits."

"Sound is the theme of the album," Paul wrote in the press release accompanying his new CD, "as much as it's about the subjects of the individual songs. If people get that, I'll be pleased." I get it, Paul. This entire book is about sound. To play music well with other musicians is to make love (figuratively) in front of witnesses. Paul's voice is thin, but it's so full of love and tenderness that its warmth is palpable. When expertly done, the dance between performer and listener is a covenant of love.

Continuing my conversation with Rhymin' Simon backstage in Nashville, I said, "I can't believe *you* remember that story!" Then I recounted the incident. "This is only the second time I've seen you perform, the first being that gig in 1968 at Forest

Hills when we opened for you and Artie. I know it's been fifty years, but I want to apologize for Jim being so rude when you came backstage to wish us good luck." Jim hadn't done anything specific to Paul, but he had exuded bad vibes.

"I remember it well," said Paul. "I was trying to figure out if he was stoned or something."

"And I was thinking," I said, "that we're never going to be successful in this business with our singer being an asshole to one-half of one of the biggest acts in music while we're just trying to get started."

"So what was going on with him?" Paul inquired.

"Jim was *always* in the stratosphere."

"Maybe he was just nervous," Paul retorted.

"Yeah, I think you're right." I'm sure that at the time Paul was thinking, *Who is this upstart?* Opening for Simon and Garfunkel had been one of our first big concerts, but even someone who eventually became a giant icon could have had cold feet.

"It reminds me of a story," Paul continued. "Back in the sixties, I loaned my apartment to a couple members of the Grateful Dead. At the time, I had an artifact, a small wooden pony from a Ferris wheel, in my pad. After a week or so, they left, and when I returned, the pony was gone. Forty years later, I ran into one of them, and he said, "Sorry about the pony." The story elicited big laughs all around.

Then I changed the subject. "Ya know, we were just a quartet. Four guys trying to carefully *listen* to each other, but now you've got nine musicians up there, each one doubling or tripling on other instruments, and it's a very tight ensemble, Paul."

"I tell them to play less . . . not too many notes," he replied.

I quickly agreed: "That's what Miles said to his musicians. I think breathing is very important."

"Yeah," Simon responded, and held out his arms for a body hug. We said our goodbyes, and both of us walked away, united by our stories from the past that had healed the present.

Chapter Twenty-Three

Ram Dass

Wheelchair Mystic

The quieter you become, the more you can hear.

Unfortunately, I met Ram Dass, the author of the best-selling "counterculture bible" *Be Here Now*, after he had his stroke. Or maybe the timing wasn't so unfortunate. As he said, "My speech was severely impaired, and I considered not speaking publicly anymore since the words came so slowly . . . but people insisted that my halting new voice enabled them to concentrate on the silence between the words." Sound familiar? The silence between the sounds of music makes the music breathe, like human beings.

I'm certainly not the fastest drummer in the world, but my exposure to all genres of music (classical, rock, blues, folk, country) has taught me to play with as much attention to dynamics as possible. Dynamics elicit the maximum emotions from the listener as well as from me. If you play with the full palette of sounds, even down to silence, you produce anger and peace and everything in between—the total human experience. Quoting Ram Dass again:

> Now that I speak more slowly, people tend to finish my sentences for me, and thus to answer questions for themselves. Though I once used silence as a teaching method, it now arises without my control and allows for a sense of emptiness, an emptiness that listeners can use as a doorway to their inner quiet. The quieter you become, the more you can hear.

Isn't that the transcendence we're all looking for? Through music, books, and art, we are trying to stop time and get a little relief from the rat race. Like Bob Marley said, there is a horse race, a human race, but this here is a rat race. Even in comedy (another art form), some of the best comedians are reaching for the same thing. In an interview, the brilliant comedian Marc Maron said to the comedic genius Gary Shandling: "I think you've changed the game with how the audience is willing to let moments *sit* with comedy. You and Rip [Torn] would just stand by the monitor [on *The Larry Sanders Show*] and nothing would be said for twenty seconds!" (And of course, in TV dead air is considered nothing short of death.)

"The *truth* actually is in the silence," Gary responded. "So coming back to the other problem in life: people are afraid to have a . . . " (Gary stopped talking for about ten seconds) " . . . silent moment like that there . . . " (he stopped *again*).

Remember, this was an interview! But Maron was right there with him.

Gary finally continued: "And in that silence right there is all the truth and all the wisdom in the world. You gotta stop talking, jumping up and giving your opinion quickly."

"Why is that?" Maron asked.

"Addiction. Addiction to preventing one to have to discover [the] true self—a defensive reaction to not having to go any deeper. Art brings these truths to the surface."

Or as the equally brilliant record producer Rick Rubin said, "Music has altered my consciousness. It takes me out of myself. You can't even put into words its effect." Art and meditation make a space where we can go deep within ourselves and find our core. Similarly, Ram Dass's silences were music to my ears.

I had met Ram Dass's sidekick, Krishna Das, who invited me to sit in with him at one of his chanting concerts. KD has become the Mick Jagger of the yoga music world. Nobody has pipes like his. Even Sting is a fan. Rick Rubin speaks of Krishna Das's voice as having an unparalleled "authority." Like me, Ram Dass and Krishna Das had their spiritual life jump-started by psychedelics, but they quickly found out that meditation and chanting offered a less shattering route. It's a longer path, but after all, we're in it for the long run, unlike our musical peers who got caught in a deep roller-coaster dive after a peak high, found the descent too steep, and bailed.

Richard Alpert (aka Ram Dass) and Jeffrey Kagel (aka Krishna Das) trooped off to India on the quintessential '60s vision quest, found their guru, Neem Karoli Baba, and gave him a megadose of LSD, to which the mystic said, "What else ya got?" Their guru had felt nothing unusual, which meant that he was already in a transcendent place. Nothing more to teach.

That was it for the two young Seekers. The devotion was immediate as the two Jewish guys from the East Coast accepted their Indian names and dropped the Torah (figuratively) right then and there. These weren't two wannabes. They endured Mother India and got a major love hit from "their teacher." Their devotion was powerful; in fact, I may be going out on a cosmic limb here, but I would say that sometimes they channel the guru.

When Krishna Das closes his eyes and opens his mouth, a trance begins for singer and listeners alike as he sings the devotional names of Indian gods in a call-and-response called Kirtan. After a long slow section (à la ragas), the tempo increases until it becomes ecstatic . . . and I mean *ecstatic*. In a tremendous outpouring of feeling, people chant, people dance, and people cry. Then there is the devastating silence afterwards, which elicits a natural high after such an outburst. Everyone in attendance feels cleansed. Just as in yoga, the real power is felt in the spaces between breaths.

KD's tabla player, Arjun (aka Alan Bruggeman), says that you can stay centered no matter what else is happening in everyday life if you keep your awareness on the space and stillness inside, which is the same as "the one" feeling of music, the rhythm in everything. This "pocket" in music is extremely important. In Ghana, for instance, only the master drummers are allowed to improvise.

I experienced this personally when I was in college. I took an African drumming class at UCLA, in the basement of Schoenberg Hall (the music building). We students stood around in a circle, playing a simple pattern on our djembes (hand drums) while the master drum teacher walked around facing each of us. Wearing a beautiful African dashiki, he locked eyes with each of us and played wild fills, trying to throw us off. None of us could hold the steady tempo. It was a great lesson. You can't solo until you've mastered the groove.

Joseph Campbell again: "The goal of life is to make your heartbeat match the beat of the universe . . . to match nature with Nature." Musicians, as well as all artists, are Seekers. They are searching for the meaning of the universe, or at least contentment and peace of mind, through sound. They know that silence is the backside of sound. If you listen to the ranting of a loud punk rock band, you need the absence of sound to take it all in.

Maybe chants and songs are a direct line to the Creator. As the songwriter Randy Newman, winner of Oscar, Grammy, and Emmy Awards, says:

How we laugh up here in heaven at the prayers you offer me
That's why I love mankind

Or as Jim Morrison said in his epic poem "An American Prayer":

O' great creator of being, grant us one more hour
to perform our art and perfect our lives.

KD's Kirtan is also kinda like a Baptist revival. My chops were challenged playing percussion with this ensemble because they never play for less than two hours and usually more,

sometimes up to three hours. And we were sitting on the floor!
But remember what I said about time disappearing.

At one gig, Ram Dass was in the back in his wheelchair,
beaming, and I asked KD if I could dedicate a poem to his pal.
Sharing a love of India in our youth and a love of playing music
(especially together), I laughed at KD's introduction of me. He
said I was someone who might have a future in the music business. I spoke to RD directly.

"Ram Dass, although this is the first time we've met, our
paths have been similar. My band took our name from one
of your peer's books: Aldous Huxley's *Doors of Perception*." I
saw RD's eyes light up back there. "I'm going to read a poem
for you by Etheridge Knight, an African American poet who
wrote this in the sixties. It's called 'Belly Song,' and it speaks of
my respect and admiration for you."

> And I and I / must admit
> that the sea in you
> has sung / to the sea / in me
> and I and I / must admit
> that the sea in me
> has fallen / in love
> with the sea in you
> because you have made something
> out of the sea
> that nearly swallowed you

I did a little hand drumming in between stanzas, which
brought some music to the reading. With the namaste head
bow, I left the stage and walked back toward my seat in the

audience. As I approached it, I realized my seat was *right next to RD!* And if I thought he was beaming before, he was on fire now! I gave him a big hug, then sat down. KD continued his performance, but the love vibe coming from next door was burning my shirtsleeve. RD's smile was so full of love that I hesitated to glance over at him because it was like getting a Shakti hit (a shot of love from the guru).

The most important lesson I learned from the man sitting next to me was to try to deal with adversity through grace and optimism. Ram Dass described his condition after the stroke as not a breakdown of concepts, but like an undressing of the concepts. "It's as if there's a dressing room where concepts got clothed in words, and that's the part of my brain that was affected by the stroke." It took him a while to realize the difference between his thinking mind, which is clear, and his verbal abilities, which are sometimes iffy. But when he did, he realized that absolutely no words are necessary. As RD said about visiting his senile aunt in the hospital, most often they just held hands and looked into each other's eyes. "We were just two beings meeting in Soul time together, and once I'd released my attachment to speaking to her on the Ego level, both of us enjoyed our visits immensely."

I was so identified with the hope that Ram Dass would acknowledge me—as the famous Doors drummer!—and validate my existence that I forgot there is something outside my feelings that is in all of us: infinity. The feeling of infinity was caught in the documentary on Ram Dass, *Fierce Grace*. In that film, the Lone Ranger (RD) was grooving in his wheelchair, with tears rolling down his face, to the music of Tonto (KD). Krishna Das had created a mood that was totally transcendental, and Ram

Dass was completely in it. It's a beautiful and moving sight, and a reminder that we all are vulnerable beings who just need love.

And what is the most direct vehicle to love? Music. It's in the air. It's not an object, like a painting, a dance performance, or a movie. With music, you can close your eyes and hear something that comes directly from one heart to another.

I realized what a blessing it was just sitting next to someone who has had some tough cards dealt to him but turned them over into joy and acceptance. It's sort of like a rehearsal for me (barring a sudden tragedy), because I'm in my seventies now and less mobility is not too far around the corner for me.

I've gotten the same feeling hanging out with Ron Kovic, another wheelchair dude. The subject of the film *Born on the Fourth of July* has a passion for life that touches everyone he meets. RD touches on this in his second book, *Still Here*, when he describes hanging out—or rolling around—with other folks who have a major disability. "I consider them among my most cherished teachers."

I was blessed to hang out a second time with Ram Dass. My girlfriend and I had lunch with Krishna Das, and we all concurred that we should try to get together once more before KD went back to the East Coast. A day or so later, he called and asked if we would like to have dinner with Ram Dass at his house! Wow! "Yes, of course!"

Driving up to RD's front door and getting out of the car was almost a Shakti in itself. Each side of the stairs leading up was strewn with sacred objects and candles. The living room had a *giant* altar to Baba (Neem Karoli Baba).

We handed off our offerings of wine and pie to RD's helpers (he has several) and then sat down. After some chitchat, the cook said that RD was already downstairs at the dinner table.

Descending wooden steps that had a ramp on the side for his electric wheelchair, we arrived at the large, square table set for twelve people. Ram Dass sat in his wheelchair at one end of the beautiful spread, the back of his beautiful, bald, head totally recognizable to us as we approached the table from behind him. I flashed on his remark in one of his books that he didn't have to worry about combing his hair anymore. (He was helping me accept my own growing bald spot!)

The assistants instructed us to look for our name cards on the table. They obviously had thought about this, because mine had been placed on the corner right next to "The Man." Ildiko, now my fiancée, was seated next to me, and Krishna Das was on the other side of RD. I broke the ice by pointing to the three of us at the end of the table: "KD, RD, and (pointing to myself) JD." This elicited a big laugh from Ram Dass, which was a relief.

Between chewing our food and RD's speech pattern, there was lots of silence. We surrendered to the evening as one long, nourishing meditation.

> I told RD that back in the day when I took acid, before I even smoked pot, LSD was still legal. I was a virgin who saw God in every leaf.
> Ildiko added that she discovered his book *Be Here Now* just when she needed it.
> As a thank-you for the meal, I offered up an excerpt from Jim Morrison's "An American Prayer," which I read while accompanying myself on tabla.
> Ram Dass told a hilarious story about taking a sitar lesson while on acid. "How did it go?" Ildiko inquired. "It was a disaster!" RD responded.

I thought of how music, when played from the heart, is a drug in and of itself, further inebriation not necessarily required.

At the end of the meal, we sat quietly for about ten minutes with the master of silence. My mind roamed away from my mantra, which Maharishi had given me fifty years ago. I thought about Pythagoras, who said that intervals between harmonious sound frequencies form simple numerical ratios. He proposed that the sun, the moon, and the planets all emit their own unique hum based on their orbital revolution, and that the quality of life on earth reflects the timbre of celestial sounds that are physically imperceptible to the human ear. Wow. My thoughts had taken me to what we were meditating on! The "music of the spheres" that can only be heard in absolute silence.

Saying our goodbyes, I gave a final note to my teacher. "Ram Dass, thank you very much. I feel calm." He reached up with his good arm to give me a "bro" handshake. It was very strong—another Shakti hit.

A year later, I was back in Ram Dass's 'hood, Haiku, Maui, with my extended family for the holidays. One afternoon, sitting on the deck of the house I rented for everybody, I said to my daughter, "See those mountains over there? How there's a valley in the middle where it looks like a 'V'?"

She nodded.

"There's a myth that some Hawaiians believe, that when they pass, they go to that valley in the mountains. It's called the 'Iao' valley."

Just then I noticed a flock of white birds fly from down near where Ram Dass lived, toward those mountains. An hour later,

I got an email from New York. It was KD, telling me that his beloved spiritual brother had passed that afternoon.

"The stroke," Ram Dass wrote, "was unbearable to the Ego, and so it pushed me into the Soul level. . . . From the soul's perspective it's been a great learning experience. Although I'm more into the spirit now, I'm also more human." Well, RD has merged entirely into spirit now, and because of his teaching, we are all more human.

Chapter Twenty-Four
Willie Nelson
Red-Headed Stranger

Young Bull Rider takes Trigger home.

S peaking of calm, this book's last sound tracker has one of the calmest set of eyes on the planet. "It's great to meet a musician who's older than me!" was my opening line to the Red-Headed Stranger.

He laughed. "Yeah, not too many of us left, huh."

My wife, Ildiko, and I had been invited to Willie's pad, where we had a very mellow afternoon.

"Have you tried this, John?" Mr. Nelson said as he handed me some of "Willie's Reserve" when we walked in the door. I was prepared. I had heard that Paul Simon and Edie Brickell had been there a few weeks earlier and left rather looped.

But being loaded worked for Willie—it fit him like a glove. It wasn't for everyone, of course, as Toby Keith sang in "I'll Never Smoke Weed with Willie Again."

"I'm a cheap high, Willie," I said taking *one* hit. Ildiko could smoke and drink me under the table, and I had no problem with that. "Why don't you two smoke for me!" I said, looking back and forth from my mate to the icon.

After being greeted with the herb, I found myself walking outside to talk to the ocean. The salt air cleared my *prana*, and I came back in with a question. "How old is that guitar of yours? As old as you?" Willie smiled as I continued. "I hate new drum heads. I like the old ones who talk back to me. They have more character."

Willie knew exactly what I meant. He had ridden Trigger (he named his guitar after Roy Rogers's horse) for a long time. Trigger was a hollow-body guitar that he was still picking on after fifty years, even though the instrument now had a hole in the front, put there when a drunk stepped on it in a club. I would say that the hole probably added to the "seasoned" sound, but the guitar's soulful tone mainly came from the picker. He used an electric pickup to get both amplification and a warm wood sound.

Once again, to musicians it's all about sound. I'm generalizing here, but country music is "warm," heavy metal is "cold," and rock 'n' roll is both, as is classical. Classical has more of the full range of sound vibrations, but all music is vibratory. It either tickles the little hairs in your ear or scares the shit out of them.

Even though he was eighty-four, my new hero still has clear blue eyes that look right through you. He's got something that

Jim Morrison was looking for in Maharishi's eyes, something I was looking for in the Dalai Lama's eyes. If Willie seems extremely mellow after a lifetime of experience, that's because it's true. Country music is known for heartbreak, and Willie has walked through it all—several divorces, an IRS seizure of his assets, four pot busts, and more. Maybe he's simply been mellow since the beginning. Maybe that's his secret.

I wanted to compliment the expert songwriter. "To me, a good song is the wedding between the lyric and the melody. I don't care if it's country, heavy metal, or pop, the way the words fit with the melody is what makes a great song. And you are a master craftsman at it." He smiled again.

"I'm gonna go down to Charlie's tonight to hear my sons' band play. Wanna come?"

Uh-oh, pressure. I had, in fact, already agreed to sit in that night with Promise of the Real, his sons' band. And now, my new mentor was going to be there too. Oh boy. Knowing this made me nervous, but also excited about the potential. After all, I had been on many stages and felt fairly comfortable there. I always said to my stomach when the butterflies came, *Yes, we're going to do it again, but it will be okay.* The butterflies had gotten smaller over the years, but I was glad they had always been there. They meant that I was risking something, that I wasn't just phoning it in, not putting on a "Vegas" act.

Ildiko and I got to the gig and were escorted to the green room, which was upstairs in the back. It had a big window overlooking the stage, and sitting in front of that window was the country music legend with his attractive and charming wife Annie. Down on the stage, Willie's son Lukas was ripping it up on electric guitar.

In the middle of the set, I went downstairs and circled around the building, making my way to the backstage. After being introduced, I said, "Well, guys, since I've never met you, and we haven't rehearsed, let's at least figure out the ending . . . in front of everybody!" Big laugh. "How about a ritard [short for "ritardando"] for the ending?" They nodded, and we started the intro to "LA Woman."

Lukas and Micah Nelson's band Promise of the Real cooked. It was real fun riding the wave of tempo changes. When I got back to the green room, everyone applauded. That felt good. "They picked the hardest Doors song ever written," I said to the man with the braided ponytail.

"But you made it through," Willie responded. That was all I needed, a tip of the hat from one of the finest songwriters ever to pick up a guitar.

Knowing that "Dad" was going to sit in for the encore with his sons' band, I asked Mr. Nelson if I could play tambourine, and he said sure. As we walked from the dressing room to the stage, lots of fans called out to him. He acknowledged everyone. Annie kept a keen eye out for weirdos, and there were a few. I gratefully sat in on tambourine as they played "Whiskey River" and "On the Road Again." It was an honor to have gotten to hang a little with one gracious, extremely talented country dude, and at the end of the night I was hoping for more.

Part II. Yes, it happened again, I got my wish. I was blessed to play some more tambourine with one of the Highwaymen (Willie plus Johnny Cash, Waylon Jennings, and Kris Kristofferson). This was at a large music festival at the beach. My squeeze and I rode on Willie's famous bus to the gig and got more hang time, as Woody Harrelson put it, with someone "everybody loves. He could be president."

I think one of the keys to Willie's longevity is humor. Even though he doesn't seem like a "young bull rider," he acts like one. Willie was firing off jokes over and over like a musical Rodney Dangerfield. He did stand-up, although he was actually sitting down. Who could blame him? His eighty-sixth birthday had been only a couple of days before.

"What's a guitar player without his instrument? Homeless!"

"What's a guitar player without his girlfriend? Single!"

And on and on. I had to add: "How can you tell if the stage is level? Look at which side of his mouth the drummer is drooling out of." An old joke, but a good one.

Then the comedian got up onstage and opened up that soulful mouth and made art. Another thing that makes Willie a master is his phrasing. Like Sinatra, he takes his time. Both singers look as though they have all day before they get to the next phrase. It seems casual, but it's dead-on accurate and totally captivating.

With most art that seems easy, a lot of work has gone into getting it to that spot. You can deliver when you're so well rehearsed that you're relaxed. As Ringo says, "It's the emotion you put into your drumming—that's the art. Leaving a hole is as important as filling it up." You have to be relaxed on some of those fast tempos or you'll get the "claw"—cramps in your muscles. Practice equals relaxation.

Back on the bus, Willie offered some ear candy. "Have you heard my new album?" he said with pride. Hitting a button on his cell, a beautiful new song from the master storyteller wafted through the bus. Called "Ride Me Back Home," it was about just that. Honoring the four-leggeds who have metaphorically carried the singer throughout life. We sat in silence, as everyone does listening to music. Music is a meditation: it gathers everyone to crouch together around a sonic campfire that crackles with healing sounds.

Instant community, that's what music creates in people, especially live music. Wherever it takes you, the life path doesn't seem so empty if it leads you through folks standing side by side, dancing, singing, and generally having a real good time.

As we exited the door of the bus, I took another chance at being Mr. Nelson's straight man. "Willie, how many times have you played 'On the Road Again'?"

"Six thousand times!" he quickly responded, laughing with a huge grin.

"That's about as many times as I played 'Light My Fire.' But they're good songs, so it never gets old, right?"

I got one final smile and eye twinkle from a beautiful, craggy face that has seen and heard it all.

Conclusion

And each name a comfortable music in the mouth,
Tending, as all music does, toward silence

—MARY OLIVER

MAYBE SILENCE IS THE GREATEST SOUND THERE IS. WITHOUT silence, we wouldn't notice sound. It's the contrast that gets our attention. So, "in the beginning" was the "word," or the Big Bang out of a dark hole of silence. A sonic vibration started everything, and it's still going. Creation doesn't seem to end.

There's been discussion recently about an apocalyptic future, but as Bob Marley said, "Have no fear for atomic energy / 'Cause none of them can stop the time." What he meant is that time will go on, time is timeless, and that's the state we get into when we sing or dance or play music. We "play" it. Music is playful, like our marine friends the dolphins, who see with sound better than we see with our eyes. Dolphins can tell the difference between a ping-pong ball and a golf ball from three hundred feet away. And they seem so joyful. The sperm whale can see a human from a mile away, using the loudest animal sounds on earth. Those sounds can penetrate through flesh, so perception of sound is 3-D for these whales. No wonder they feel like kindred creatures. In some ways, they're smarter than us.

Before Gustavo Dudamel puts his ecstatic hands in the air to break the silence with a gorgeous symphony, there is the black hole of no sound. The poor Beatles had to quit playing live early in their career because the fans were screaming before they had played even the first note of music, depriving them of the contrast between sound and silence.

One thing that unites all of the brilliant artists discussed in this book is being ahead of the curve. Theirs is a lonely road; they are always having to wait for the public to catch up. Bob Dylan said that his audiences are always three to five years behind. While that might be true in his case, other artists' audiences may be only a couple of years behind in understanding them, and others are six feet under when the light of admiration finally turns on.

In Martin Scorsese's film documentary on Dylan's Rolling Thunder Revue, he asks the greatest songwriter of the century what he is searching for. Scorsese quotes Hurricane Carter, the subject of one of Bob's songs: every time Hurricane sees Dylan, he asks the songwriter if he's found what he's looking for. Dylan says, "Yes, it's the Holy Grail."

In other words, Dylan is looking for something so elusive that he will be searching for it the rest of his life. That's the key to creativity, not pursuing the goal of giant audiences or millions of hit records. The path is where the excitement is. And in that spirit, anyone can find that road.

Another thing that gifted musicians and artists have in common is their ability to make it look easy. And believe me, it's "looks" only. Behind the effort are the years of perfecting their craft, or perfecting their lyrics—writing tons and tons of sentences only to use a few and throw out the rest. The ease comes from sweat, from the many, many hours in the "sauna" of honing their craft (not to mention sometimes sweating onstage in front of everybody). When I'm home intently listening to music, I sweat. I imagine playing drums along with the composition, or I imagine a different arrangement, and that makes me sweat. Maybe when you're trying to do something new, sweat is a requirement.

Certainly in physical activity, pushing the envelope produces sweat, as do even less rigorous artistic endeavors if the concentration is intense. Maybe new ideas act as an agent for physical cleansing. Maybe when you're really tortured trying to incubate a new idea, your sweating lubricates its birth.

For me, an artist's incubation period is the most special time. Lightbulbs are flashing continually with new ideas, and the energy is electric. It is a precious period, and difficult to return to. I've been blessed to have been able to witness an incubation time with several of the great artists discussed in this book. I was there when the walls shook in Shelly's Manne Hole jazz club from the churning rhythms driven by my idol Elvin Jones under Coltrane's horn. It was as if his drumsticks were kindling, lighting an even larger fire to cook John's melodies into a perfect meal. Then I saw Janis and Marley and Van Morrison in their early days. And of course, I rode the train out of the station with Jim Morrison. You could feel the coal being shoveled into that engine.

Sadly, this period must pass when success comes fast. In America, we seem quick to co-opt an artist; we want more of the same magic and leave the artist no time to produce the slow, perfectly cooked feast. Some musicians try to rekindle that first incubation period by going back to their roots, but it's the rare artist who can pull it off. Most just duplicate what brought them success in the first place.

Gustavo Dudamel has managed to reach back to his youth as a young conductor by organizing Youth Orchestra Los Angeles (YOLA). YOLA mirrors Gustavo's musical schooling in El Sistema in Venezuela. When I asked the Maestro if conducting YOLA has affected his conducting of the LA Philharmonic, he said, "Definitely. It's as if I've gone back to my childhood, dipping into the energy, connecting with the original fire that made me passionate about music in the first place."

One reason why The Doors succeeded in reaching back was that we did not accommodate ourselves to technology. We recorded on eight-track because the newer sixteen-track recording machines wouldn't fit in our rehearsal room, where we wanted to record. Eight-track was limiting, but because we didn't want to leave the place where we felt at home, the place where we originally jammed together, it worked. The result was *LA Woman*, a comeback album that seems to endure.

The gift that all these troubadours have received for the hours and hours they have spent focused on honing their vision is time. It disappears. Whether you're rehearsing an orchestra, leading a rock band, or sitting alone in a room staring at a blank page or a blank canvas, a space comes up if you're really in it. Certainly some drugs expand time, but pure concentration on a craft will get you as high as a martini—with no hangover! Well, that's not entirely true. You're left hungover with a lifetime desire to have more of that space.

Years ago in an interview, Bob Dylan was asked if he was happy. He wouldn't answer the question. He intuitively knew that to have soul is to have what the Brazilians call *saudade*, or "longing."

On the back of *Riders on the Storm* is a quote from Oliver Stone: he called me "a survivor and a seeker." The code to the Grail is to stay open and keep learning. And continuing to ask questions, no matter what your age, seems to be a way to stay young, or at least young at heart. You can keep having "peak" moments because, as Bob Dylan knows, there's no final big answer, just a road paved with wonder.

Professional musician or not, we are all Seekers. So make room every day for your practice (music, painting, mindful walking, whatever gives you space), and you will receive the balance needed for that day's challenges. In tumultuous times such as these in America in the early twenty-first century, the soul appreciates the chance to tap into the infinite sources of creativity that can be accessed in any situation. Just being mindful can be creative.

The mythologist Michael Meade tells of a tribe whose members wake up at dawn to sing their dreams to each other, because "they imagine that they are participating in the eternal reverberations of the song of creation, and the sound of existence that is pouring into the world." Furthermore, they imagine the living word of creation to be a continuing resonance and a resounding vibration inside each person's life.

Music touches something very deep. The idea is that if songs (people's stories) don't get out into the world, folks lose their direction in life. Even if your artistic endeavors are only for yourself, it gets out. Do it. The reggae group Steel Pulse (in many ways the heirs to The Wailers) wrote, "Life without music I can't go." Anyone's life can be a song. We don't all have to "make the charts." To quote possibly the most brilliant LP ever made, by the transcendental Stevie Wonder, what is your "song in the key of life"? The poet Rumi puts it even more succinctly:

Without you the instruments would die.
Your breath is needed, your voice is required.
Either lend your breath to the song, or else leave us alone,
For we have been drafted as instru-
ments in the essential fight for love.

To get lost in something you love—that's the ticket. It doesn't have to be writing a symphony. It can be doing something that no one will ever see or hear, but in "the moment" when you're doing it, infinity creeps in.

Carl Jung said that man has a thirst for the eternal. I hope these mentors of mine have quenched some of that thirst for you. I for one feel satiated for the moment, but I know I won't stay in that moment, that I will become thirsty again soon.

For now, though, I want to close with a big thank-you to the folks I've written about. I thank them because, whether famous or not so famous, these musicians and artists have given us a gift. They have shared one of the secrets to making life easier: *a touch of sonic seasoning turns a meal from bland to delicious.* I also know that, wherever they are, our admiration will feed them in turn. That's how it works: the relationship is reciprocal.

What do my mentors have in common? Looking past the trappings of each artist's sound and each artist's culture, we can see the deep humanity inherent to all types of music. All of us are made of flesh and bone, heart and soul, and we share the same experience of driving, walking, or running down the road from birth to death. Whether we're traveling on the German autobahn or an Appalachian dirt path, our experience is the same; we have embarked on a journey of spirit in our human bodies as we proceed down our path on Planet Earth. And music is a candle, lighting the way along the road toward the art of living.

Blessings,
John Densmore

Permissions

"Break on Through to the Other Side"
Words and Music by John Densmore, Robby Krieger, Ray Manzarek, and Jim Morrison
Copyright © 1967 Doors Music Company, LLC
Copyright Renewed
All Rights Administered by Wixen Music Publishing, Inc.
All Rights Reserved. Used by Permission.
Reprinted by permission of Hal Leonard LLC

"God's Song (That's Why I Love Mankind)"
Words and Music by Randy Newman
Copyright © 1970, 1975 (Copyrights Renewed) WC Music Corp. and Randy Newman Music
All Rights Administered by WC Music Corp.
All Rights Reserved
Used by Permission of Alfred Music

"National Book Award Speech" by Robert Bly
Used by permission of the author.

"Night Frogs" by Robert Bly.
Used by permission of the author.

"Pisces Fish"
Words and Music by George Harrison
Copyright © 2002 Umlaut Corporation
All Rights Reserved
Reprinted by permission of Hal Leonard LLC

"Today, like every other day"
From *Rumi: The Book of Love: Poems of Ecstasy and Longing* by Jalal al-Din Rumi, translated by Coleman Barks.
Used by permission of the translator.

"The Way It Is" by William Stafford from *Ask Me: 100 Essential Poems*
Copyright © 1977, 2014 by William Stafford and the Estate of William Stafford
Used with the permission of The Permissions Company, LLC, on behalf of Kim Stafford and Graywolf Press, Minneapolis, Minnesota, graywolfpress.org.

Index